TRANSCENDING VISION

Christian Theology in an Age of Empiricism

DON McINTOSH

GERIZIM · HOUSTON

Transcending Vision
Christian Theology in an Age of Empiricism

© 2018 Don McIntosh
Gerizim Publishing, Houston, Texas
www.gerizimpublishing.com

ISBN-13: 978-0692121146
ISBN-10: 0692121145

Cover photo by Pixabay. Used by permission.

All rights reserved. No part of this publication may be reproduced, stored in a retrieval system, or transmitted, in any form or by any means, electronic, mechanical, photocopying, recording or otherwise without the permission of the author.

Unless otherwise noted, Scripture references are from the New King James Version of the Holy Bible. Copyright © 1982, Thomas Nelson, Inc. Used by permission. All rights reserved.

Dedicated to:

All who have lost their vision of heaven
Because their sights are fixed on earth.

Contents

Foreword by Dr. Ernest Musekiwa   7
Preface   11
Introduction   13

I. Outlines of Christian Theology

1. Laying the Foundations: Axioms of Christian Theology   21
2. Theology Proper: Divine Attributes and the Trinity   29
3. Christology: Son of God and Son of Man   57
4. Soteriology: Many Called, Few Chosen   71
5. Eschatology: The Present and Future Kingdom   81

II. Instantiations of Christian Theology

6. Building on the Foundations: A Study of 1 Cor. 3:1-15   95
7. And the Word Was God: A Study of John 1:1-18   107
8. Theology at the Fringes: Miracles, Dreams and Visions   117
9. Theology Beyond the Fringes: Heresies in History   131
10. The Human Condition and the Hope of the Gospel   177

"Where there is no vision, the people perish."
– Proverbs 29:18, KJV

"Write the vision…that he may run who reads it."
– Habakkuk 2:2

"I was not disobedient to the heavenly vision."
– Acts 26:19

Foreword by Dr. Ernest Musekiwa

I consider it a wonderful privilege to introduce this book, *Transcending Vision: Christian Theology in an Age of Empiricism* by my friend and colleague Don McIntosh. As a Christian minister for over two decades and a Christian educator, I have rarely come across such fine books that have shaped and sharpened my theological worldview. Over the years, several books have appeared highlighting the events and misgivings of the churches of their generations. Some writers have been spiritually gifted to pierce through the veil and discover some very essential elements that, if observed, can spur a greater reformation and revival in our churches. In our day, Don's is one such voice that has risen in the church, calling it back to a renewed zeal, commitment, and passion for its Lord.

But why write such a book in a world where countless Christian books already exist? This book is a must read because it calls every believer to rise up and be the Christian God desires. Don has done a great work in helping the church open its eyes to see the reality and urgency of the hour. I believe this book is a passionate plea, a heart cry for revival in our generation that seeks to reach every person in the church, the learned and unschooled, the theologian and the laity, in simple language that all can understand. As Don makes it clear throughout the book, his qualifications are based in God and his ministry reaches out to *all in the church,* not just a few elites but the "common people."

In recent decades, the Christian faith has come under intense attack from humanists, atheists, philosophers of all categories, and even those in other religions. Christianity's unique claim that Jesus Christ is God and the only way of salvation has been in the theological melting pot of several religions. Just recently, there were complaints from Christians that the Google Home device does not know who Jesus Christ is. Social media sites try to suppress the spread of the Christian message. In several Asian and African countries, the church is under severe persecution. The church's foes are many, from within and from without. However, the Lord Jesus Christ has said clearly of the church: "The gates of hades will not prevail against it" (Matthew 16:18). Don writes from this perspective. He believes that the church should be sound in the faith and should be aware of what is at stake.

Thus, his presentation of the essential framework of biblical doctrines in a fresh way will help you to reconsider, reexamine and review what is at stake in the church in light of the coming apostasy. Without being equipped and prepared to stand against the schemes of the enemy in this generation, the church will suffer innumerable fatalities. Thus, the book you hold in your hands is sent forth with the expectation of helping you be sound and strong in the faith, with a pure vision of who God is and what He wants to do.

The first section considers four of the most misunderstood topics and rarely preached or taught doctrines in most churches. It is evident to me in my discussions with students and other fellow believers, that there is a great dearth of teaching in these areas. I am glad that Don has provided just the material needed. Sometimes believers are intimidated by theological books filled with theological jargon; but this work is easy to read and easy to understand.

The second section seeks to help us understand some theological ideas as they are set forth from the Scriptures and contemporary contexts. Without building on Christ, "the author and finisher of our faith" (Hebrews 12:2) who is "the hope of glory" (Colossians 1:27), the Christian faith is of no value. Don and I both believe that the current mushrooming of heresies and poor presentations of the gospel have contributed to a loss of vision, which is a serious stumbling block to an effective witness of the church. Hence, this book is a wake-up call, not only to reexamine our faith but to live lives worthy of the gospel in anticipation of the soon coming King of kings and Lord of lords.

It is with great honor that I commend this book to you, dear reader, so that your faith may be strengthened as we "grow in the grace and knowledge of our Lord and Savior Jesus Christ." (2 Peter 3:18). To the end, we will be established in truth and be rooted in Christ. You may not agree with all the points raised by the author, but be sure of this one thing: this is a passionate plea to the body of Christ to catch the vision and keep it renewed and transcending. Without vision, the people perish. Our generation should not perish; nor should the next generation, when such timely messages can stir us into action.

As we approach the end times, the world becomes more hopeless and only the church has the answers. Without the church's presence in this world, the world is utterly doomed, bound to despair. Hence, we should be able to see beyond our modern religious and political spheres with the understanding that God has made us divine partakers of His nature. The earth and everything in the world belongs to the Lord (Psalm 24:1), and knowing God is the greatest achievement one can obtain in this world. The Lord Jesus Christ, not some modern "gods" conceived in the minds of corrupt men, has to be enthroned in every man's heart. Only those of the divine nature are able to bring a fresh vision of hope and life to a hopeless world, and only if they themselves have gotten hold of a transcending vision of who God is and what He desires of us.

Ernest Musekiwa, Th.D., Ph.D.
Author, *Evangelism: The Unfinished Task*
President, Christian Missions Theological College & Seminary
Harare, Zimbabwe

Preface

There appears to be a great need these days for fresh spiritual vision. From everything I can gather we have become a nation, a culture, so given over to the material pursuits of wealth, entertainment, social media interactions, sex, food, and other sources of immediate gratification, that many of us have lost the ability to envision possibilities beyond the realm of our immediate, visible experience – let alone to apprehend the reality of God. Apparently underlying this spiritual shortsightedness is a fascination, even reverence, for empirical science and technology.

My reason for writing is that I believe Christian theology has the potential to correct this situation. Now let me say up front that I have not offered treatments on every major aspect of theology; neither have I addressed all the specific subdomains of theology: ecclesiology, hamartiology, missiology, pneumatology, or various other "-ologies." Nor have I made clear demarcations between systematic, biblical, historical, dogmatic, exegetical, philosophical, pastoral or apologetic theology (let alone tangents like political theology or liberation theology). All these fall under the general rubric of Christian theology.

For disclosure's sake I should also mention that I am not a professional scholar. While I honestly don't believe academic credentials are required to write, preach, teach, exposit Scripture, or otherwise minister effectively, I do understand that they matter to many people. They don't matter to me so much – or at least they shouldn't – because I know that my calling and equipping are ultimately from God and not from men. Like Paul, I don't believe myself in need of "letters of commendation" from the scholarly community to minister in the Word and doctrine. In my view the demand for credentials among ministers in the church is a holdover from the traditional clergy-laity distinction that was never supported by Scripture in the first place. We would do well here to recall that the essence of discipleship is *learning* (as opposed to *knowing*), and that the disciples of Jesus were mostly unlettered tradesmen.

The Lord is faithful to direct my steps. So it is that I happen to enjoy my place in the kingdom of God as a "layman" minister of the gospel, doing my part to edify the church, sharing the good news of the kingdom and the resurrection of Jesus with the people in my community (when I can find the time and the boldness anyway), writing books like this one, working a secular job to support my family and contribute to the general welfare, and otherwise glorifying God in whatever way I can. Besides, with all my reading and knowledge-gathering I would rather not get too far removed from the humble testimony of Christ: "The common people heard Him gladly" (Mark 12:37).

All this is not to diminish the blessings of formal training (I do have a Master of Divinity degree under my belt, and I recently started work in a Doctor of Apologetics program). Indeed, this book could not have been written apart from the wise, patient instruction of some highly knowledgeable instructors who have contributed to my own theological education, especially Dr. Johnson C. Philip at Trinity Graduate School and Dr. Derek Morphew at the Vineyard Institute. (Much of the content of this book has been developed from my coursework at both schools.) Also I am blessed and honored that my friend Dr. Ernest Musekiwa, President of Christian Missions Theological College in Zimbabwe and African Director of Triune Biblical University, has graciously agreed to review the book and write a Foreword.

As much as men like these have inspired me, I would be remiss not to mention three other people in my life who inspire me even more. I will say again what I say every day in my prayers: I am so thankful to God for my beautiful wife Tricia and my children Vance and Chloe. What a great blessing they are to me!

With all that said, I encourage readers to discover and embrace a fresh, theologically informed vision of who God is and what he might be saying in our day: *"Lift up your eyes and see..."*

Don McIntosh

Introduction

Theology has fallen on hard times. During its glory days in the High Middle Ages, theology was known as the "Queen of the Sciences," owing to its undisputedly central role in medieval society. Although it is true that theology, or at least theologians, often slipped into obscure metaphysical quests far removed from both common life and the Scriptures, it was understood by all that God himself was the foundational reality that explained everything else. Human institutions and experiences, the law, the arts and the sciences – all had their ultimate justification in a Christian conception of God.

That all changed with the battles over epistemology[1] during the Enlightenment. Between the *rationalists*, with their vaunted "first principles" of logic and metaphysics, and the *empiricists*, lovers of science given to skepticism of anything not perceptible to the senses, traditional theology found itself slowly squeezed out of the public consciousness. Theology became obsolete at the same time that doubt became fashionable. In many quarters, especially the university, theology simply never recovered. Today's thoroughly secularized students would likely find it hard to believe that earning a degree at great universities like Harvard and Princeton at one time required coursework in theology as part of the core curriculum.

The situation is not that much better in the church. While there is certainly an abundance of "teaching" offered up from countless pulpits, there appears to be little in the way of an established theological understanding or ground rules of interpretation in place to help guide the effort. Theologians like Robert H. King suggest that as a result of all this, "theology is in a state of disarray," especially on the systematic front: "[T]here

---

[1] "Defined narrowly, epistemology is the study of knowledge and justified belief… Understood more broadly, epistemology is about issues having to do with the creation and dissemination of knowledge in particular areas of inquiry." – from Matthias Steup, "Epistemology," *Stanford Encyclopedia of Philosophy* (Fall 2017), Edward N. Zalta, ed., <https://plato.stanford.edu/archives/fall2017/entries/epistemology/.>.

is no general agreement even as to what theology is, much less how to get on with the task of systematics."[2]

The way I see it, the present funk in which so many theologians now find themselves can be explained by empiricism basically winning the aforementioned epistemological conflict. In secular societies such as ours, where religion is mostly privatized and natural science is held to be (far and away) the most reliable source of knowledge, empiricism has emerged the dominant epistemology. Now by "empiricism" I don't mean so much the old Enlightenment view that sense experiences cast impressions on the mind which themselves constitute knowledge; but the more modest and seemingly more widely accepted claim that knowledge *begins* with sense experience, and from there is refined and expanded through various tools and methodologies of science.

Under this new and improved version of empiricism the presumption that science holds the key to knowledge is very strong, not only among moderns but postmoderns. J. P. Moreland describes a widely held view of the world that seems to accept postmodernism in all areas of inquiry *except* the hard sciences, a view he calls "axiological postmodernism" and behind which stands

> an implicit epistemology that we may call *folk empiricism*, which holds that *for any belief P, P is reasonable to believe and assert if and only if P can be and has been adequately tested with one's five senses*. Let's name this claim FE. The point of FE is to limit what we can reasonably believe and assert to what can be "appropriately" tested with the five senses, and the hard sciences are taken to be the best exemplars of this epistemic standpoint.[3]

---

[2] Robert H. King, "Introduction: The Task of Theology," in Peter H. Hodgson & Robert H. King, eds., *Christian Theology: An Introduction to its Traditions and Tasks* (Minneapolis: Fortress Press, 1994), p. 1.

[3] J.P. Moreland, "Four Degrees of Postmodernism," in Paul Copan & William Lane Craig, eds., *Come Let Us Reason: New Essays in Christian Apologetics* (Nashville: B&H Publishing Group, 2012), p. 31.

Alan Musgrave seems to agree with Moreland on this point: "Science... teaches us that perception is a more or less indirect process: the perceiver is separated from the object perceived in space and time, and is linked to it by a more or less elaborate causal process, rather than being in direct 'contact' with it."[4] So the new knowledge criterion is not so much direct perception, but scientific testability.

Conversely, any proposition *not* scientifically testable is now considered suspect, perhaps the product of personal biases. The irony here is that the preoccupation with all things scientific is itself a bias. This fact may have something to do with the predominance of STEM (Science, Technology, Engineering, Math) subjects over and against the humanities in higher education. In universities, like anywhere else money is exchanged for goods and services, subjective human desires, preferences and perceptions of utility create demand for the products which others are eager to supply.

I would argue, then, that there is more to explain the rise of this "new empiricism" or "folk empiricism" – hence the decline of religious faith – in public life than the material successes of science and technology. At the heart of empiricism is a moral-spiritual crisis, a failure (or refusal) to acknowledge God as Creator and Jesus Christ as Savior. A relatively recent (2015) *Pew Research* study reveals that despite maintaining its relative dominance over the domestic religious landscape, Christianity (or in any case the kind of Christianity that actually affects moral decision making) is evidently in serious decline in the U.S., while unbelief appears to be on the rise:

> But the major new survey of more than 35,000 Americans...finds that the percentage of adults (ages 18 and older) who describe themselves as Christians has dropped by nearly eight percentage points in just seven years, from 78.4% in an equally massive Pew Research survey in 2007 to 70.6% in 2014. Over the same period, the percentage of Americans who are religiously unaffiliated – describing

---

[4] Alan Musgrave, *Common Sense, Science and Scepticism: A Historical Introduction to the Theory of Knowledge* (New York: Cambridge University Press, 1999), p. 92.

themselves as atheist, agnostic or "nothing in particular" – has jumped more than six points, from 16.1% to 22.8%....[5]

Various other studies have suggested that in statistical terms the above referenced "adults who describe themselves as Christians" in America behave almost exactly like everyone else in the country, in that they (or *we*, I should say) are just as likely to commit a crime, cheat on a spouse, or abort a child. Meanwhile our zeal has clearly faded. Church involvement, prayer, charitable giving and personal evangelism have all taken a serious hit in recent decades. Every indication suggests that America has almost completely squandered the priceless spiritual capital she inherited from Christianity at the founding.

As I write this, our nation is reeling from yet another mass school shooting and again looking to political leaders for answers. I would respectfully suggest that the problem derives not from a lack of "common sense gun legislation" but a loss of spiritual vision. The book of Proverbs declares famously that "Where there is no vision, the people perish" (Prov. 29:18, KJV). Other translations have, "...the people cast off restraint," or, "...the people lose control."

This principle appears in keeping with the biblical assessment of the violent, chaotic times of the Judges – "In those days there was no king in Israel; everyone did what was right in his own eyes" (Judg. 17:6) – and of the life of Samuel: "And the Word of the Lord was rare in those days; there was no widespread revelation." (1 Sam. 3:1). The idea seems to be that a lack of spiritual vision, i.e. a failure to apprehend or envision God, or the spiritual realm, or for that matter anything else beyond our present earthbound experience, correlates with a certain noxious lawlessness. A vicious cycle sets in, where loss of vision results in loss of moral, spiritual, and psychological well-being, and vice-versa.

In firing what some would consider the unofficial first shot in the modern debate over political correctness, the 1987 publication of *The Closing of the American Mind*, philosopher Allan Bloom argued that

---

[5] "America's Changing Religious Landscape," *Pew Research Center* (2015) <http://www.pewforum.org/2015/05/12/americas-changing-religious-landscape/>.

(post)modern culture, largely the product of institutions of higher learning, had sacrificed its spiritual, moral and intellectual life to the exigencies of positivistic science and worldly sensuality. Bloom thus stressed the importance of actively reading books (rather than passively listening to music or watching television), particularly the classics, and remarked: "The failure to read good books both enfeebles our vision and strengthens our most fatal tendency – the belief that the here and now is all there is."[6] Of course, the Bible is commonly known as "*the* good book." And it could be argued that "the belief that the here and now is all there is" amounts to a rough definition of empiricism.

Obviously having vision is important. Just as important, however, is the *content* of the vision. Here it should be pointed out that theology is not simply *doctrine* – where doctrine is understood as something like "a set of beliefs required for salvation or membership in the body of Christ." To be certain, theology has its instructional, doctrinal and dogmatic functions, and these are essential for the life and health of the church. Paul reminds us that without sound teaching we are easily "tossed to and fro and carried about with every wind of doctrine" (Eph. 4:14). But theology also *inspires* – or it should. In the current "age of information" this inspirational aspect of theology can easily be lost or undervalued. We students of the Scriptures too often forget that the Word of God consists not only of doctrine, but of promises, prophecies, accounts of courage and heroism, and motivational calls to rise up, do battle and take the land. This book has been written, then, not merely to inform but to inspire.

---

[6] Allan Bloom, *The Closing of the American Mind: How Higher Education Has Failed Democracy and Impoverished the Souls of Today's Students* (New York: Simon & Schuster, 1987), p. 64.

I. Outlines of Christian Theology

1. Laying the Foundations: Axioms of Christian Theology

In a society that many would describe as post-Enlightenment, or post-modern, one of the unfortunate lingering effects of Enlightenment modernism is an obsession with *epistemology*, that navel-gazing branch of philosophy dedicated to the study of knowledge and its justifications. (Clearly not everyone is a fan; historian Will Durant once wrote off epistemology as simply "that dismal science.") Among the many philosophers and theologians who do maintain interest in the subject, most would agree that the proper aim of such epistemological efforts, dry as they may be, is the identification and justification of true belief. And as any student of epistemology will attest, that task turns out to be much more difficult than it might sound.

Although there are two main theories for how knowledge is structured – *foundationalism* and *coherentism* – most philosophers consider themselves foundationalists, meaning that they hold all knowledge to be built up from a certain unshakable "foundation" of properly basic beliefs. Now these beliefs are said to be *properly* basic because they are logically self-evident, incorrigible[7], or directly perceived by the senses, so that they need no justification of their own.

The Foundation of Faith

However, it should be noted not only that these basic beliefs appear to need no justification, but that they *cannot* be justified, say by appeal to an even more basic or more foundational belief. While basic beliefs are eminently useful for proving the truth of various propositions, then, they cannot themselves be proven. They can only be *accepted* as true. In a sense the modernist epistemology project has therefore come full circle: at one time having discarded the ancient faith of our forefathers as essentially so

---

[7] An "incorrigible" belief is said to be one that really cannot be false from the standpoint of the believer – for example my belief, when I feel hunger pangs, that I am indeed hungry.

much naïve, unscientific superstition or cultural baggage, modern epistemology has come to recognize that ultimately nothing can be known apart from belief. It could be said that belief "fills the gap" between our valid logical intuitions and reliable sense experiences, and knowledge. Or as the book of Hebrews has it, "Faith is...the evidence of things not seen" (11:1). It turns out that sophisticated modern theories of knowledge are not that far removed from Scripture.[8]

In other words, foundationalism works when we accept *beliefs qua beliefs*. Christian theology accepts that faith is foundational, and for that reason it may be argued that theology actually coheres better with our understanding of reality (and the ultimate non-provability of its truths) than the much more ambitious but unsuccessful empiricist or positivist programs. I have argued elsewhere that this insight is consistent not only with human experience but even the most formal of the sciences, mathematics: "As Kurt Gödel demonstrated with his celebrated incompleteness theorems, most any consistent, formal system is capable of generating true statements that nonetheless cannot be proven within that system."[9]

Of course, many people are not comfortable with the idea of resting knowledge on a foundation of "belief." The logical positivists of the previous century, for instance, held that knowledge can legitimately arise by only two means: empirical verification and logical soundness. But their program was eventually found to be self-defeating. Basically, it turned out that the "verification criterion" – the belief that any proposition must be either logically self-evident or empirically verifiable to hold meaning – was itself neither logically self-evident nor empirically verifiable.

According to Alvin Plantinga, a similar problem faces foundationalism itself, what he calls *classical foundationalism* (CF). CF has found itself in "self-referentially hot water," he says, because

---

[8] Bock, for example, describes himself as both a "critical realist" (in acknowledging the external world and its intelligibility) and a "biblical foundationalist" (in accepting certain ground-level truths, beginning with the Scriptures, that can only be held by faith) – see Darrell L. Bock, *Purpose-Directed Theology* (Downers Grove, IL: Intervarsity, 2002), pp. 23-26.

[9] Don McIntosh, *Transcending Proof: In Defense of Christian Theism* (Houston: Christian Cadre, 2016), p. 59.

there don't seem to be any incorrigible or self-evident propositions that support CF itself. It certainly isn't self-evident; it isn't such that anyone who understands it can just see it to be true. For example, I understand it, and I don't see it to be true. In fact I believe it to be false...Furthermore, CF isn't incorrigible; it isn't at all about how things appear or seem to anyone. And still further, it certainly doesn't look as if there is a good argument for CF from propositions that are either self-evident or incorrigible...Accordingly, CF seems to be self-referentially incoherent.[10]

To roughly restate the problem: we cannot *know* a truth if we are not at the same time willing to *believe* it. Our most reliable means of acquiring knowledge usually depend upon certain seemingly self-evident truths: axioms of probability theory, axioms of set theory, rules of logic, assumptions of the scientific method, and so forth. But as noted above, these axioms cannot be proven, only believed. What, then, are some of the basic theological beliefs – foundations of the faith – that could be expected to reliably inform Christian theology?

At this point Christian theologians might begin with the recognition of Scripture itself as the self-attesting revelation of God. Closely related would be the common philosophical observation that God exists as a (or rather *the only*) necessary being, or that God is the "ground of being." Others might appeal to God's essential attributes, such as omnipotence, immanence, immutability, righteousness, holiness, love, grace, etc. As a Christian believer I want to begin where the New Testament begins. Paul the apostle declared that "No other foundation can anyone lay than that which is laid, which is Jesus Christ" (1 Cor. 3:11). Theologian Michael Bird argues, "We do not open our theological project with bibliology or a doctrine of Scripture since that would make reasoning from Scripture our foundation, whereas the foundation for our knowledge of God is God himself..."[11] "Apart from Me," said Jesus, "you can do nothing" (John 15:5).

---

[10] Alvin Plantinga, *Knowledge and Christian Belief* (Grand Rapids, MI: Eerdmans, 2015), p. 15.

[11] Michael F. Bird, *Evangelical Theology: A Biblical and Systematic Introduction* (Grand Rapids, MI: Zondervan, 2013), p. 93.

Our Creator and Savior, Jesus Christ, "the Word made flesh," is himself our theological foundation.

But beyond the revelation of Jesus himself, Christian theologians from as early as the second century have sought to establish certain theological dogmas (*axioms*, in a sense), as baseline truths upon which others might be formulated and against which others might be compared. The Apostles' Creed would be a notable summation of these:

1. I believe in God the Father, Almighty, Maker of heaven and earth:
2. And in Jesus Christ, his only begotten Son, our Lord:
3. Who was conceived by the Holy Ghost, born of the Virgin Mary:
4. Suffered under Pontius Pilate; was crucified, dead and buried: He descended into hell:
5. The third day he rose again from the dead:
6. He ascended into heaven, and sits at the right hand of God the Father Almighty:
7. From thence he shall come to judge the quick and the dead:
8. I believe in the Holy Ghost:
9. I believe in the holy catholic church: the communion of saints:
10. The forgiveness of sins:
11. The resurrection of the body:
12. And the life everlasting. Amen.[12]

Together these truths constitute a set of "essentials" that define and circumscribe sound doctrine. Notice that these dogmas are preceded by "I believe." Without believing, we cannot know God. But as mentioned earlier, without believing neither can we know anything else.

Faith and Rationality

That brings us to another holdover from the Enlightenment, namely the myth of a "conflict" between faith and reason. In the previous decade the so-called "New Atheists" made much of this alleged tension, extolling

---

[12] "Apostles' Creed," *Christian Classics Ethereal Library*, <https://www.ccel.org/creeds/apostles.creed.html>.

scientific rationality and at the same time maligning religion as a "virus of the mind." Faith, they argued, is little more than the refusal of adults to give up their cherished childhood beliefs. The presumed faith-reason dichotomy appears to underlie the related, and equally presumed, conflict between science and religion. One must choose between faith or religion, and between reason or science, because in each case the two categories are, again presumably, mutually exclusive. Uncritical acceptance of this proposition usually leads to either scientific naturalism (atheism, essentially) or *fideism*, i.e., a faith with no rational justification.

Against both scientific naturalism and fideism, the foundational truths of the gospel are found between two epistemological extremes: reliance on reason alone and reliance on revelation alone. In today's largely irrational, postmodern culture, however, it is sometimes supposed (not only by atheists and critics but the faithful themselves) that faith is a strictly "religious" belief that disregards and even despises reason. Even highly educated, leading Christian philosophers like William P. Alston and Alvin Plantinga have often appeared to undermine the role of reason in an attempt to make peace with their atheist critics.

Rightly understood, Christian faith is more than an arbitrary belief, but is always grounded in a spiritually compelling, divinely ordered and inspired, historically attested revelation of truth. Here confusion may arise from reading faith to be strictly separate from "sight," or empirical observation, when in fact faith also serves a sort of *inferential* purpose, as a means to knowledge that rests upon a reliable foundation of evidence and experience of God.

Frequently in the Scriptures the Greek words *pistis* (faith) and *gnosis* (knowledge) find mention in the same statement to describe complete understanding, as in John 6:69: "...we have *believed and known* that you are the holy one of God..." Other times faith is presented as a form of knowledge based on testimony or the witnessing of a miracle. In that sense faith is something much like an inductive inference. Consider the appeal to evidence made by Jesus himself: "Believe Me that I am in the Father and the Father in Me, or else believe Me for the sake of the works themselves" (John 14:11). The "works" referenced here encompass all that Christ did to glorify the Father, including public miracles and exorcisms (and later his resurrection from the dead). These works constitute evidence pointing to the divinity of Jesus. So faith is not simply "beyond" the confines of knowledge; rather it is a kind of knowledge itself, founded on divine revelation and attested by empirical evidence.

According to Christian apologist Dick Sztanyo, knowledge comes to us through various avenues, the first four of which are: *induction* (wherein specific truths suggest a general conclusion), *deduction* (general truths lead to a specific conclusion), *empirical data* (direct observation), and *credible testimony*.[13] This latter source of knowledge gets short shrift among secular philosophers and intellectuals, but the fact is that most of what we recognize as *knowledge* is "passed down" through the testimony of trusted human authorities. Almost all of what a typical student learns at the university, for instance, comes by way of textbooks rather than through lab experiments or field observations.

At issue here is what Sztanyo calls "the believability and defensibility of the gospel." Current concepts of faith unfortunately have their roots in skeptical philosophy rather than the testimony of Scripture. In the *Critique of Pure Reason*, Kant defined faith as antithetical to knowledge (though necessary for moral advancement). Kierkegaard suggested that faith is an existential "leap in the dark" toward God. William James, ever the pragmatist, presented faith as a "hypothesis" which offers more practical "cash value" than unbelief. At the heart of all these notions is the conviction that Christianity may be relatively probable, but never proven. Against this, the apostles declared the resurrection of Jesus to be a fact of history, so that the truth of Christianity can be proven beyond a reasonable doubt. Although beliefs and convictions cannot be forced upon us apart from an acknowledgement of the will, it remains clear that the main tenets of the Christian faith rest upon a firm foundation of truth revealed in history, and can be accepted by faith as certain.

A number of biblical texts openly promote a rational view of faith. In 1 Peter 3:15, the famous "apologist's verse," Peter makes rational defense of the gospel a Christian obligation, to "always be ready to give a defense to everyone who asks you a reason for the hope that is in you." 1 Thess. 5:21 challenges believers to "prove all things," or test every claim

---

[13] Dick Sztanyo, *Faith and Reason* (Montgomery, AL: Apologetics Press, 1996), p. 3. Much of the material in this chapter is drawn from Sztanyo's insightful analysis of Christian epistemology.

for its empirical and rational validity. In Acts 17, Luke confers a certain nobility on the Bereans, who examine Scripture in light of reason. Paul in Philippians describes his calling as a Christian in terms of "defense and confirmation of the gospel" (1:7), that is, a life dedicated to setting forth the truth of God in reasonable and understandable terms. In the Old Testament, Isaiah speaks for God in challenging the false gods and their promoters to "bring forth strong reasons" to substantiate their beliefs against the fulfilled prophetic claims of the God of Israel (Isa. 41:21). He appeals directly to evidence.

Faith and Fideism

In the New Testament, salvation comes by faith in Christ. To believe "in" Christ suffices to justify a man and make him righteous in the eyes of God through the imputed righteousness of Christ. However, faith in God can scarcely be maintained for long if doubts subsist as to the existence or reality of its object. In other words, Sztanyo suggests, "psychological certitude" (spiritual conviction) needs to be accompanied by "intellectual certainty" (rational validity) if cognitive dissonance, or at least cognitive instability, is to be avoided. As Paul noted in 1 Cor. 15, there is ultimately no point in exercising faith in the resurrection if in fact the resurrection has not taken place.

Contrary to these sensible suppositions, fideism upholds faith as a virtue precisely *because* it thrives in the utter absence of evidence. Faith is therefore little more than – as William James put it – "The Will to Believe." Popular as fideistic notions of faith may be, they stand against the far more reasonable depiction of faith in Scripture. It could be said that fideism has more in common with agnosticism than with Christian faith. Agnosticism, after all, declares that no one can have knowledge of God; fideism merely adds to that claim a determination to go ahead and believe anyway. Fideism is faith without an epistemic foundation, which leaves it arbitrary and irrational. All this amounts to another good reason for identifying and affirming the axioms of Christian theology (and for Christians to receive some training in apologetics).

Sztanyo maintains that faith is properly understood as "volitional commitment of an informed intellect." Nonetheless, he says, alternative "hypotheses" for the relationship between faith and reason abound. These include: (1) *The "as if" hypothesis*. This approach holds that, since articles of faith can never be validated, they must be treated on a conjectural basis. Of course, if faith's object cannot be validated, the basis for exercising faith disappears, and Christianity becomes a strictly subjective, personal matter. (2) *The probability hypothesis*. Here the believer is said to grasp biblical truth only as a sort of best bet, on the likelihood of its being true. Of course, "probably true" also means "not necessarily true," and therefore is incompatible with the absolute truth embodied by Jesus Christ. (3) *The "leap of faith" hypothesis*. This popular position holds that the believer follows the evidence as far as it will allow, and then takes a metaphysical leap to close the remaining distance. Faith in this case is volitional but lacking intellectual and epistemic vigor. Each of these positions implicitly denies that the object of faith represents at the same time an object of knowledge. Yet as mentioned, the Bible frequently synthesizes these two concepts. Jesus is to be both believed and known.

In light of the preceding, it should be clear that an understanding of epistemology is essential for Christians facing a growing host of technical philosophical questions and seeking a rational response. But I need to throw in a caveat: whereas biblical faith is eminently reasonable, faith is not simply the handmaid or extension of reason. Christians often must "keep the faith" even when irrational doubts arise in their own hearts, or when some form of logic appears to temporarily point in the way of unbelief. It would be a shame (not to mention an eternal tragedy) if disciples of Christ abandoned their commitments every time their own understanding of logic or initial interpretation of evidence led them to doubt.

Jesus died for all men and calls us to "Repent and believe the gospel" (Mark 1:15). He does not call us to process the gospel intellectually and then decide whether or not to believe it. The truth of the gospel is rational to believe, yes, precisely because it is self-attestingly true. But rationality and intellectualism cannot save us. According to the New Testament we are saved *through* faith, *in* Christ, *by* his grace – which means we are not saved by faith-plus-works, nor for that matter by faith-plus-logic, nor even faith-plus-evidence. I would again argue, therefore, that the ultimate foundation of Christian epistemology remains the authority of Jesus Christ, the living Word, revealed through Scripture.

2. Theology Proper: Divine Attributes and the Trinity

From the fall of man to the present, idolatry has been a serious stumbling block for the people of God. Believers throughout the ages have found themselves continually confronted with the temptation to create God in their own image, or at minimum to present him in culturally acceptable terms. So it is that twenty-first century Christians often seem to understand God to be what is basically "left over" after all the facts of science and secularism have been acknowledged. What remains is little more than an idol concocted in a secularized imagination – not a proper object of faith at all. For this reason and others it would benefit Christians – and I don't mean just theology students – to undertake a careful study of the nature and attributes of the godhead. This is our high calling, to know God and glory in him (John 17:3; 2 Cor. 10:17).

From a practical standpoint, a biblical study of God himself (also known as *theology proper*) is the best way to know God – to know his character, plans and purposes. Though we cannot see the invisible God, a study of his attributes reveals him to us. Given that God constitutes the foundation of human morality, understanding God's character also reveals what sort of character *we* should have as his disciples. To misunderstand or redefine God in terms other than his own self-revelation is idolatry, which leads quickly to sin and judgment. Knowing God is ultimately our highest calling as Christians, that we might become "partakers of the divine nature" (2 Pet. 1:4). Knowing God enhances our worship, our prayer life, our witness, and our grasp of related spiritual truths. Kenny Rhodes says simply, "The importance of the doctrine of God cannot be overstated. It is the bedrock of all theological understanding… It is the doctrine upon which all other doctrines must be judged and articulated."[14]

A potential problem that emerges at this point is the seeming disconnect, at least in certain respects, between the God described by the philosophers (or the God of "classical theism") and the God depicted in Scripture. Whereas the God of the philosophers – Aquinas chief among

---

[14] Kenny Rhodes, *The One Who Is: The Doctrine and Existence of God* (Bloomington, IN: Westbow Press, 2015), p. 10.

them – is defined by a number of abstract, transcendent perfections (omnipotence, eternality, immutability, simplicity, etc.), the God of Scripture appears personally and even emotionally interactive (like in the story of Jonah) in such a way that the two conceptions are not easily reconciled. Eleonore Stump explains:

> That is because, on classical theism as it is often interpreted, God is immutable, eternal, and simple, devoid of all potentiality, incapable of any passivity, and inaccessible to human knowledge. So described, the God of classical theism seems very different from the God of the Bible.[15]

Despite this tension Stump makes the case, after carefully unpacking the meanings of the divine attributes from Aquinas' own perspective, that the God of classical theism and the God of the Bible are actually "the same God." They are the same "not because the biblical God is after all a frozen and unresponsive deity, but because the God of classical theism is truly the engaged, responsive, intimately present God of the biblical stories, in whose image human beings are made."[16] For Aquinas and countless others the classical-theist picture of God does not precede study of the Bible, but follows from it.

In Scripture, the revelation of God is not only deeply personal but frighteningly powerful. An encounter with God is usually profoundly life-changing. Job's revelation of God in the whirlwind, as case in point, sparked deep humility and trembling repentance. Moses realized, even if slowly and reluctantly, that God is an eternal, holy, all-knowing and all-powerful Deity. Once he came to this realization, Moses insisted that God's presence go with the Israelites in their journeys (Ex. 33).

This all leaves us with both good news and bad. The good news is that God desires to fellowship with men, and has made the means available. The bad news is that God is holy and will not stand sin in his presence – yet all have sinned. God owes us nothing, and we owe him everything.

---

[15] Eleonore Stump, *The God of the Bible and the God of the Philosophers* (Milwaukee: Marquette University Press, 2016), p. 18.

[16] Stump, p. 109.

It could be argued therefore that of the attributes to be discussed below, *grace* is the basis for any further insights we may hope to gain as humans into the saving nature and character of God.

Divine attributes are often distinguished as either *communicable* or *incommunicable*. Says Michael Bird, "The incommunicable attributes refer to those elements of God's being and character that are unique to himself and cannot be shared with others. The communicable attributes... are transferable and shareable with others in limited degrees."[17] It may be helpful to observe further that the incommunicable attributes are roughly equivalent to the attributes of God in classical theism.

Omnipotence

One of those incommunicable attributes is *omnipotence*. Skeptics and critics often seize upon such limitless "omni" characteristics and hold them up for ridicule. Omnipotence is said to be nonsensical, in that if God can do *any-thing*, he should be able to do absurd things like pop in and out of existence or create a stone too heavy for him to lift. Because these scenarios are incoherent, as the objection goes, so is the doctrine of omnipotence. To this I would answer simply that God has all possible or *real* power. He does not have impossible or *unreal* power. If skeptics really want to insist that God should also have illogical or unreal power, then they should be consistent and not appeal to alleged logical incoherence in theism as a justification for unbelief.

Drawing from Anselm's meditations in the *Proslogion*, McGrath observes that omnipotence, wrongly understood, would also permit God to be selfish and unjust. "Yet this is clearly inconsistent with the Christian understanding of the nature of God. The concept of divine omnipotence must therefore be modified by the Christian understanding of the divine nature and character."[18] I tried not long ago to make the same basic point in an online rebuttal to Dan Barker:

---

[17] Bird, p. 127.

[18] Alister McGrath, *Christian Theology: An Introduction* (Malden, MA: John Wiley & Sons, 2001), p. 282.

Concepts do not perfectly convey definitions; to the contrary, definitions imperfectly convey concepts. To misunderstand this is to reduce substantive reasoning to quibbling, and lend credence to logical fallacies such as equivocation.... Here "omnipotence" does mean "all power," but not in a zero-sum sense. "All power," at least in theological terms, means unlimited capacity on the part of God to do whatever he chooses. The former definition precludes free will. The latter does not.... God is not shackled by definitions of words coined in order to describe him in the first place.[19]

God has displayed his power in a variety of ways. Obviously the earliest such display was the creation of the universe. As Paul argued, the power of God is "clearly seen" via creation (Rom. 1:20). David in the Psalms likewise affirmed the testimony of creation to God's power: "The heavens declare the glory of God..." (Ps. 19:1). The other commonly cited proof of God's power is the Exodus, by which God brought the mighty Egyptians to their knees and liberated his own people from bondage. Jeremiah noted both elements in his prayer and acknowledgment of God's power: "Thou hast made the heavens and the earth by thy great power .... Thou didst bring thy people Israel out of the land of Egypt with signs and wonders..." (Jer. 32:17-24).

Emphasis on the power of God remains just as strong in the New Testament. Jesus made the power of God the proof of his messiahship to John the Baptist in prison: "...the blind receive sight, the lepers are cleansed, the deaf hear, and the dead are raised..." (Matt. 11:4-6). Jesus healed every affliction, from the physical to the emotional and spiritual (Luke 4:18-19). The greatest sign of his power is the resurrection, or "the sign of Jonah," who was swallowed up for three days and then released to life again. The final sign will be the return of Christ, when every eye will see the risen one in glory.

A word should be added here about *omniscience,* the understanding that God knows everything, or more properly, that God knows everything that is knowable. "He knows all things" (1 John 3:20). More properly still,

---

[19] Don McIntosh, "Is God Incoherent? A Reply to Dan Barker," *Cadre Comments* [blog], August 24, 2016, ttp://christiancadre.blogspot.com/2016/08/is-god-incoherent-reply-to-dan-barker.html>.

according to scholars like Rhodes, "God does not have knowledge. He is knowledge." This is because, according to classical theology, "God is a most simple being."[20] Often omnipotence and omniscience are distinguished to address the issues particular to each. For our purposes we will assume that omniscience falls under the domain of omnipotence. Given that omnipotence is the state of having all possible power, and that knowing is a possible power that can be had in varying degrees, it seems to follow that omnipotence entails omniscience. In the same way, omniscience seems to follow from God's immanence or omnipresence. If all of reality is immediately accessible to God, then God also knows everything that can be known.

A belief in the truth of omnipotence inspires reverence and honor towards God, a faith that laughs at the impossible, and a confidence that personal weakness cannot limit divine purposes. Indeed, in Scripture God only moves *through* the weak and the broken, that he might alone receive the glory (2 Cor. 4:7). Throughout the New Testament, God's power is said to be working in the believer continuously, toward ends beyond our present comprehension (Eph. 1; Col. 1:29; Rom. 8:8-11; etc.). This outlook should lead us to a serious, expectant prayer life, a confidence to stand down demonic powers, and a willingness to obey even through deep sufferings.

Eternality

Another of the incommunicable attributes of God is eternality, which relates closely to God's self-existence or *aseity*. "He is factually and logically necessary; it is impossible that He could ever have come into existence and impossible that He should ever go out of existence."[21] The Psalmist declares, "Even from everlasting to everlasting, You are God" (Ps. 90:2). As creatures trapped in time we are clearly limited in our understandings and descriptions of eternity. Although some thinkers, e.g., Richard Swinburne, regard eternity as unbounded time, others find eternity best expressed as a dimension technically *outside* the world marked

---

[20] Rhodes, p. 178.

[21] Rhodes, p. 161.

by time, but which causally relates to that world in a special way. Eleonore Stump has argued that "Because the mode of existence of an eternal God is characterized by a limitless and atemporal kind of presentness, the relation between an eternal God and anything in time has to be one of simultaneity." There is a point, the *eternal present*, at which God acts simultaneously "between what is eternal and what is temporal."[22] Recognizing the difficulty of describing this relation, Stump compares our situation to that of a creature inhabiting a strictly two-dimensional world, "Flatland," and trying to describe its interaction with a visitor from the three-dimensional world.

Temporal-eternal interactions must therefore appear mysterious or miraculous to an earthly observer in time. Rhodes adds that the mystery of an eternal God relating to temporal humanity "has been the occasion for heretical doctrines like Open Theism and process theology.... God is not a being like us, but He transcends all creaturely confinements and categories."[23] Christians are called to worship God as who he is, and God is not just another creature trying to find his way in the physical universe. At the same time we can draw great encouragement from the fact that God is everlasting, and that his kingdom endures forever. The promise that we will be raised to life by the same Spirit that raised Jesus (Rom. 8:11) means that we will partake of his eternal blessedness. "And they shall reign forever and ever" (Rev. 22:5).

Immanence

Children often ask, "Where is God?" More often than not they are told in reply, "God is everywhere." And so he is. At the very beginning, before Adam and Eve fell into sin, God and his people walked together in undisturbed harmony, God being tangibly near. Even after the fall, God remained true to his nature and therefore remained close to Adam and Eve by covering them with animal skins and thereby enacting atonement as part of his larger plan of redemption. God determined to close the distance between humanity and himself that sin produced.

---

[22] Stump, p. 61.

[23] Rhodes, p. 166.

During the Exodus event, God drew near to the Israelites and preserved them from the plagues, from the vengeance of Pharaoh, and from the perils of the wilderness – despite their complaints. As the people understood quite correctly, the presence of God is not a comfort but a terror to sinful men; but through the intercession of Moses and the assurances of God himself, the Israelites learned to appreciate his grace, and thereby appreciate his presence.

The immanence, or omnipresence, of God is a central theme of both the Psalms and the prophets. Psalm 139, especially, elaborates on the reality of God's nearness, as David consoles himself that no one can escape from the presence of God. The prophets urged the people not only to recognize God's nearness, but to draw near themselves for the sake of their own sanctification. In the presence of God empty professions become reverent acts of worship and thanksgiving. Conversely, failure to draw near resulted in condemnation. Israel suffered reproach, for "She did not trust in the Lord; she did not draw near to God" (Zeph. 3:2).

The New Testament equally speaks to this nearness. As the book of Hebrews exhorts, believers are now called to "draw near in full assurance of faith." Believers take comfort in the fact that we may "draw near with boldness" to the throne of grace (Heb. 4:15). God's presence, opened up by the work of Christ on the cross, now provides joy and assurance to the anxious, as testified in numerous passages (Eph. 2; 1 Thess. 4; Rev. 21). God draws near most powerfully today through the active ministry of the Holy Spirit (John 14, 16). Because it's such a blessing, the presence of God is the essence of the promise of heaven (Rev. 21, 22).

Immutability

As the world increasingly confronts us with moral chaos, political turbulence and rapid expansion of technology we can take comfort in realizing that God is essentially unchanging. "He is not one who would change his mind" (1 Sam 15:29). This "unchangeableness" of God is known as *immutability*, which Rhodes defines as "the denial of any kind of change, either substantial or accidental, in God. God is immutable (unchanging) in His being, perfections, promises, and purposes."[24]

---

[24] Rhodes, p. 167.

Immutability is not just a comfort to the believer but a hazard to the unbeliever, since God will certainly judge sin at the same time that he will assuredly be true to his promise of forgiveness: "For I am the Lord, I do not change; therefore you are not consumed, O sons of Jacob" (Mal. 3:6). This also speaks to Christ's divinity, because only God is immutable and yet the New Testament ascribes this quality to the Son: "Jesus Christ is the same yesterday, today, and forever" (Heb. 13:8).

The doctrine of immutability provides an encouragement for New Testament saints, who worship the only God "with whom there is no variation or shadow of turning" (James 1:17). For this reason we may be confident that God will continually work "all things together for good" for his own (Rom. 8:28). This doctrine ensures our "imperishable" hope in the everlasting realm of eternity. God's eternal kingdom, "a kingdom which cannot be shaken" (Heb. 12:28), is possible only because God is and always will be. At the same time, immutability speaks of God's character, and is therefore a trait worthy of emulation in the church. We ourselves should strive for steadfastness of faith and constancy of purpose.

Love

Of the "communicable" attributes (those shared and understood to some degree by men), love is probably the most important. The love of God is a central tenet of Christian theology, yet has been tragically misunderstood by many. Whereas some believe in a vengeful or indifferent deity with no real concern for humans at all, others embrace a god of permissive "free love" who abandons justice and accountability altogether. Therefore a need exists to understand God's love.

Love is the overriding motivation for God's great acts of redemptive history, culminating in the sacrifice of Christ (John 3:16). Love is equally the standard to be embraced by all believers in their own lives (1 Cor. 13). So important is love that Jesus declared it to be the summation of all the Law and the Prophets. Accordingly, Christians should pursue the virtue of love with great diligence. From an evangelistic and apologetic standpoint, love in the life of a believer is strong *evidence* of a heart transformed by the living God.

God's love is distinct, unlike that of any other being. It is infinite and unfathomable, so that we only get tastes and glimpses of the great love

God has for us. It is eternal, an "everlasting love" (Jer. 31:3). Along the same lines, the love of God is inseparable from his very nature, hence immutable. John sees a virtual equivalence: "God is love" (1 John 4:16). This is an "unchanging love" (Mic. 7:18), without variation (Jas 1:17). In that love is the preeminent virtue of God that defines not only his being but his acts, all this suggests an important point of contact between biblical theology and classical theism on the issue of divine simplicity.[25] Love is the all-consuming nature of God.

That said, love by definition cannot be or act in isolation. Love is always relational, and therefore must relate to an object or recipient. So Donald Guthrie comments on the love of God in 1 John:

> It is clear that John is not expounding a merely ontological characteristic of God, a quality locked up in the heart of God. Indeed, it may be questioned whether such an abstract form of love is conceivable.... The fact that so much is made in John's gospel of the Father's love for the Son is a strong indication that it is within the Godhead that God's love has an object.[26]

This Trinitarian interrelationship explains how God can love even prior to the creation of the world of creatures like ourselves.

However, God's love is also inextricable from his holiness and righteousness. Blamelessness and holiness are found with God in love (Eph. 1:4). God loves all men unconditionally, but such love cannot harbor or condone sin. Love, then, points to the cross, where God poured out wrath upon all the sins of men, through Christ, so that he could pour out his love

---

[25] James Dolezal says, "The classical doctrine of simplicity, as espoused by both traditional Thomists and the Reformed scholastics, famously holds forth the maxim that there is nothing in God that is not God. If there were, that is, if God were not ontologically identical with all that is in him, then something other than God himself would be needed to account for his existence, essence, and attributes." – *God Without Parts: Divine Simplicity and the Metaphysics of God's Absoluteness* (Eugene, OR: Pickwick, 2011), p. xvii.

[26] Donald Guthrie, *New Testament Theology* (Downer's Grove, IL: Intervarsity, 1981), p. 105.

upon humanity. Thus God's love is sacrificial, abandoning self-interest for the interests of others. This is a personal, individually-focused, heartfelt love, not a technical requirement for being divine or a broad-brushed general feeling toward mankind.[27] Still, for anyone who doubts God's love for men, the cross stands as proof positive: "God so loved the world that he gave his only begotten Son." The forgiveness of God, so vital to our salvation and our psychological health, derives from love.

Closely related to God's love is his forgiving nature. Forgiveness lies at the very heart of the gospel, and can be seen in the revelation of Christ to the disciples on the road to Emmaus: "that repentance for forgiveness of sins would be proclaimed in his name to all nations" (Luke 24:47). The Old Testament describes God as "compassionate and gracious, slow to anger, and abounding in lovingkindness and truth" (Ex. 34:5-7). The good news for anyone who has felt the condemnation of sin and failure is that "To the Lord God belong compassion and forgiveness" (Dan. 9:9).

Because all have sinned, and the wages of sin is death, mankind faces a serious problem apart from forgiveness. "The soul who sins will die" (Ezek. 18). Since the fall in the Garden, mankind has stood in need of God's forgiveness and the hope it represents. The problem of sin points to the reconciliation of the cross, for only God can forgive sins committed by men. Furthermore, only God can transform the heart, for is out of man's own corrupt heart that sin inevitably proceeds. The law is fair, or as Paul said, "holy and just and good." Sadly, it serves to expose the corruption of the human heart.

For this reason, God has not called men to become good. He knows they cannot. Rather, he calls men to *believe* upon him for righteousness, by faith. This appeal to faith explains how Joshua could declare that the commandments of God are "not too difficult." By faith alone the righteousness of the law can be obtained. This is the essence of the New Covenant: forgiveness of sins through Christ.

---

[27] According to Calvinists, God's love is an act of sovereign selection, so that God chooses to love some and reject others in order to demonstrate his glory. This leads naturally to the doctrine of "limited atonement": that Christ died only for the elect. But Christ was driven to the cross by love (John 3:16), not by a longing to manifest his glory. If God loves us this is not due to God's whims, much less our "lovability," but God's own loving nature.

Because Christ shed his blood for us, we are forgiven. "There is no longer any offering for sin" on the part of men (Heb. 10:18). "In him we have redemption through his blood, the forgiveness of sins, according to the riches of his grace" (Eph. 1:7). This is the gospel, good news indeed; but it ought to be received with considerable reverence, for the not-so-good news is that God will reject those who reject his forgiveness.

Goodness

From the creation to the final judgment, Scripture consistently describes God as good and the only source of goodness (Psalm 16; James 1:17; etc.). One of the best sources of insight into God's goodness is Psalm 73, in which Asaph the Psalmist initially questions the worthiness of the life of faith, hence questions the goodness of God. Through a revelation of God's character and eternal plan, Asaph realizes that goodness is far more than a short-term experience of pleasure or a trouble-free life, but is found in the presence of God. Because God is himself goodness, the "good life" can only be had in proximity to him. Job learned the same lesson at the end of his trial with the appearance of God in the whirlwind.

For some, though, the goodness of God is logically, and therefore *theologically*, problematic. In the *Euthyphro*, Plato framed the problem basically like this: is something good because God wills it, or does God will it because it is good?[28] If good is defined as what God wills, good seems to be an arbitrary determination of the Deity. But if God wills what is already good in itself, it seems that God is subject to a higher, external standard of goodness. In this way the "Euthyphro dilemma" seems to undercut Christian theology.

Yet the Euthyphro may be a false dilemma entirely. If God's very *essence* is goodness, it may be that God merely wills what is consistent with his own essence. Why shouldn't he? Of course, someone could still object that God has "arbitrarily" or "subjectively" decided that his own goodness is inherently legitimate, but what they really seem to be saying is that intrinsic goodness, i.e., the truth of moral realism, is impossible. (What would make an external standard of morality stick, anyway?) And

---

[28] Or as Plato has it originally: "Is the pious loved by the gods because it is pious, or is it pious because it is loved by the gods?" – *Plato's Euthyphro* (New York: American Book Co., 1902), p. 17.

that doesn't seem to follow from the fact that the concepts of God and goodness seem to overlap in some way. For much the same reason we may observe that true propositions are logically sound, and logically sound propositions true, without fretting too much about which – truth or logical soundness – ultimately grounds the other.

God's goodness means that we are secure in his faithfulness and promises (Rom. 8:28), and that God is good even in the midst of hardship and suffering. In short, God is always good, and the gospel is always good news for men. For me this basic understanding provides an "anchor for the soul" (Heb. 6:14) that strengthens faith and inspires a genuine optimism in the purposes of God, along with a resolve to draw nearer to him in faith.

Wisdom

Wisdom is a sublime characteristic that easily eludes men. After all, human beings by nature are not wise, but foolish. As both the Proverbs and the apostles declare, "Wisdom is from above." Wisdom involves not only moral ideals and attributes but the "know how" to live them. Ever since the fall, man has habitually made the mistake of confusing "knowing good and evil" with simply recognizing the distinction between the two. But wisdom transcends mere intellectualism or academic knowledge; it ascertains the understanding of what leads to godliness and eternal life. Paul instructed believers to "be wise in what is good, and innocent in what is evil" (Rom. 16:19). When men try to experience the best of both they get nothing but frustration and corruption. We must therefore distinguish between true and false wisdom. One is given by God; the other is rooted in pride and self-interest (James 1). One leads to life; the other to a corrupted knowledge of good and evil.

Unfortunately, the fascination with science and technology in the current social climate has led to the replacement of wisdom with technical knowledge. What garners awe and respect is no longer people of diligence, integrity and courage, but technocrats who know how to write code, solve complex equations and manipulate financial systems. Success is measured strictly in terms of dollars and degrees. God's wisdom has nothing to do with this tech-savvy, worldly intellectualism.

The wisdom of God has been manifested in numerous ways, first through the nation of Israel. Paul's examination of God's careful treatment of Israel in Romans concludes by celebrating "the depth of the riches both of the wisdom and knowledge of God" (11:30-32). Through Israel, God has brought light to the Gentiles, who in turn have provoked Israel to jealousy by their faith in Christ, "so that all may be saved." God alone has the prescience, vision and insight to devise such a plan. Elsewhere Paul indicates that God has revealed his wisdom through the church. Over the long term of history, God is working in and through the church for his glory and for the salvation of souls. Like the conductor of a grand opera, God orchestrates events to accomplish his own wise purposes.

Holiness

For most Christians, the resurrection of Christ is proof of God's power. But the resurrection is equally a vindication of Christ's holiness. Because he was "without spot or blemish," Jesus was able to escape the judgment of death. Holiness means to be distinct or uniquely separated, and for this reason only Christ the Son qualifies among men. "There is none holy like the Lord..." (1 Sam 2:2). Holiness implies moral purity, a complete innocence of any wrong or sin. This is so much the essence of God's character that the angels continually describe God as "holy, holy, holy." One source defines *holiness* as

> The attribute of a being that entirely fulfills the purpose of its existence and is thus at one with itself. Strictly speaking, only God is holy, as being "the awesome and fascinating mystery" (*mysterium tremendum et fascinans*), "utterly other" than human beings and indescribably holy (see Is 6:3, 5) and yet the source of all our spiritual and moral perfection.[29]

This is important to understand, for holiness cannot be defiled or compromised. Thus God takes it quite seriously when his holiness is transgressed, impugned, or scorned by his people. The examples of Moses striking the rock in the desert and Uzzah taking hold of the ark of God both demonstrate God's absolute intolerance for overt breaches of his holiness. In both cases the presence of God was lightly regarded, and resulted in

---

[29] Gerald O'Collins and Edward G. Farrugia, *A Concise Dictionary of Theology* (Mahwah, NJ: Paulist Press, 2000), p. 107.

punishment. Holiness ought to inspire reverence. Isaiah stood in the presence of God and immediately realized the depth of his own sinfulness, so that the angel cleansed him with a touch to his lips of a hot coal from the altar. The lesson seems to be that holiness is from God, not men, and consequently any fruitfulness we experience derives from God alone (1 Cor. 3:1-7; 2 Cor. 2-6).

Holiness has been revealed firsthand in the person of Jesus Christ. Jesus was set apart in holiness even before birth, so that he was born of a virgin by the Holy Spirit (Luke 1:35). The testimony of those who observed him was consistently, "This man is innocent," and "This man was the Son of God" (Luke 23:47; Mt. 27:54). Acts repeatedly calls Jesus "the Holy One" (2:23-27; 13:32-35). Holiness is additionally a high obligation for the church to embrace. Without reverence for God's holiness, men tempt Christ to wrath and literally drink judgment upon themselves (Acts 5; 1 Cor. 11). Irreverence occurs when men fail to recall or recognize the holiness of God. Unless we pursue his holiness we cannot see the Lord (Heb. 12:14). In her pursuit of holiness the church can appreciate reverence for God above personal self-esteem. Holiness also inspires genuine, heartfelt, reverent worship. Finally, a revelation of God's holiness sparks repentance in the church and makes it clear that the gospel is the only way to liberate men from the bondage of sin.

Righteousness

Although closely related to the idea of holiness, righteousness means something more like conformity to a standard in dealings with others. However, God cannot be held to a standard; rather he sets the standard in his own nature. The righteousness of God therefore speaks to the justice, rightness, fairness and equity inherent in God's nature. Abraham came to the revelation of God's righteousness through the judgment of Sodom, not only in discovering the heart of God to spare the righteous and judge the wicked, but in his own accessibility to God's grace in the process.

To Israel, God showed his righteousness by revealing his will and Word. Through instruction, correction, and predictive prophecy, God speaks what is necessary for men to believe and be saved. Israel in turn becomes a light to the Gentiles. God reveals his righteousness generally by instructing men in the Word, by fulfilling his promises, and by judging the enemies of Israel. God rains judgment on the wicked at the same time that he steps in to protect the poor and lift up the humble. Righteousness is not merely "love," or "justice," but the two flowing together from the heart of God.

In the New Testament, righteousness becomes the center of controversy. Jesus declared that the righteousness of participants in the kingdom of God would exceed that of the scribes and Pharisees. This came as a shock to the Pharisees, as well as others who upheld them as the guardians of the Law. Righteousness is a matter of the heart. To the extent it can be seen, righteousness exhibits lowliness and humility rather than ostentation and pride (Matt. 5:3-11). As the issue involves the heart, the practice of exhibitionism and showmanship in the name of religion was consistently condemned by Christ (Matt. 6:1; 7:15-23).

Righteousness is essential to salvation, because one is saved by participating in the righteousness of Christ by faith. This is *imputed*, but nonetheless very real and efficacious righteousness. "God is just and the justifier of the one who has faith in Jesus" (Rom. 3:26). For these reasons, faith is the highest virtue – the only *saving* virtue – and self-righteousness the most lethal of sins.

There is an unfortunate flip side to the righteousness of God, namely his wrath. In light of God's righteousness, and the sin and rebellion of men, the wrath of God ought to come as no surprise. When men malign God's character and disparage his Word, righteous indignation, or wrath, is the result. This explains why the Israelites in the wilderness, griping and committing idolatry in unbelief, so often came under the wrath of God. For their part, the Israelites were to be instruments of God's wrath against a perverse and idolatrous Canaanite nation (Deut. 7:1, 2). Without committing themselves to war against Canaan, Israel would be doomed to spiritual corruption and judgment themselves, as the book of Judges attests.

The wrath so prominently featured in the Old Testament carries into the New Testament, where John the Baptist warns repeatedly of "the wrath to come" and one aspect of the ministry of Jesus is *propitiation* – literally the appeasement or satisfaction of God's holy wrath. It's important here to emphasize the future aspect of wrath, as Jesus made clear that suffering in this lifetime need not imply displeasure on the part of God. Thus, when John says that "the wrath of God abides" upon the unbeliever, he refers to future, final judgment.

How is God's wrath reconciled with his love? Well, the one really follows from the other, in that human disobedience and idolatry provoke divine jealousy, which in turn incites the wrath of God. "You shall worship no other god, for the Lord, whose name is Jealous, is a jealous God" (Ex. 34:14). God only becomes jealous for us when we fall into the arms of another god because his love for us is intense. Or as Guthrie has it, "Some concept of wrath is needed to safeguard the purity of divine love."[30] Here is another reason to think that God is best known and understood in personal, relational terms. The wrath of God induces a wise and healthy fear of God and deep appreciation for the blood of Christ that has changed us from "children of wrath" to children of God.

Grace

To the surprise of many unfamiliar with the Old Testament, God's grace has been demonstrated powerfully from the very creation and ever since. To Moses, God revealed himself as "compassionate and gracious, slow to anger, abounding in lovingkindness and truth." Jacob discovered God's grace the hard way, having wrestled with God and broken his hip only to find that it was by God's grace alone that he could find the blessing he sought. Jonah's story also highlights the grace of God, as God uses the selfishness and sanctimony of the wayward prophet to demonstrate his own grace to seemingly hardened and incorrigible unbelievers. Jonah despised his own discomfort, but worse, despised the grace of God extended to the unwashed sinners.

Of course, grace has been manifested most powerfully in the person of Jesus Christ. The words, healing ministry, and sacrificial death of Jesus all attest loudly to the grace of God. In a sense, grace is the dividing line between faith and unbelief, life and death. After all, believers appreciate grace as much as the self-righteous despise it. Grace becomes a stumbling block to the self-assured. The good news of the gospel is all about grace, that whereas all have sinned and fall short of God's glory, all are "justified freely by his redemption through the grace that is in Christ Jesus" (Rom. 3:23, 24). Such grace is not of ourselves; "it is the gift of God" (Eph. 2:8).

---

[30] Guthrie, p. 103.

However, one of the central paradoxes of Christianity is that this freely bestowed grace has become available to us only at a high cost, namely the death of the Son of God on a cross of crucifixion. For this reason Christianity knows nothing of "cheap grace," as Dietrich Bonhoeffer famously put it:

> Cheap grace means grace as a doctrine, a principle, a system.... An intellectual assent to that idea is held to be of itself sufficient to secure remission of sins. The Church which holds the correct doctrine of grace has, it is supposed, *ipso facto* a part in that grace.... Cheap grace means the justification of sin without the justification of the sinner.[31]

Or as Paul has it, "What shall we say then? Shall we continue in sin that grace may abound? Certainly not! How shall we who died to sin live any longer in it? (Rom. 6:1-2). To the one who entertains the idea of sinning freely through the presumed license of grace, the Spirit warns: "For if we sin willfully after we have received the knowledge of the truth, there no longer remains a sacrifice for sins, but a certain fearful expectation of judgment..." (Heb. 10:26). Such a cavalier attitude amounts to holding the blood of Christ with contempt (Heb. 10:29).

Hiddenness

Invisibility, or hiddenness, may seem a relatively unimportant dimension of God's character, and worse, in contradiction with passages describing God's appearance to men. After all, Scripture says that "No man has seen God at any time" (John 1:18) and yet also declares, "I have seen God face to face" (Gen. 32:30). This seeming inconsistency is dispelled when we consider God's self-disclosure in various forms (sometimes as a man, as an angel, or as a voice from heaven) – none of which can fully capture God's majesty and glory. All we get on this earth is a partial glimpse of the incomparable eternal reality. God reveals himself only in part, because for a man to gaze upon the complete fullness of God would be fatal. He dwells in "unapproachable light" (1 Tim 6:16).

---

[31] Dietrich Bonhoeffer, *The Cost of Discipleship* (New York: Touchstone, 1995), p. 43. First published 1959 by SCM Press Ltd.

Thus a certain hiddenness results from the tension between the human and divine aspects of Christ's own character. His divine and human natures are not quantities to be measured within Jesus, so that more of one means less of another, but are complimentary aspects of the being and character of Christ. The eternal Word dwelt in human flesh (John 1:14). To see Jesus is to see God, in a sense, but because Jesus has "emptied himself" in becoming a man, there is far more to the glory of God than what can be seen in the physical person of Jesus. Thus Jesus had to explicitly pray for his name to be glorified, because his appearance was not inherently glorious (John 17).

Skeptics have appealed to hiddenness as the basis of a relatively new and apparently sophisticated argument against theism. Given that God is perfectly good, and that belief in God is a requirement for salvation and happiness, one might argue that a perceived failure on the part of this perfectly good God to reveal himself is itself grounds for unbelief. Schellenberg presents the broad outlines of his version of the argument from hiddenness as follows:

> A perfectly loving God would desire a reciprocal personal relationship always to obtain between himself and every human being capable of it. But a logically necessary condition of such Divine-human reciprocity is human belief in Divine existence. Hence a perfectly loving God would have reason to ensure that everyone capable of such belief...was in possession of evidence sufficient to bring it about that such belief was formed. But the evidence available to us is not of this sort....[32]

My own take on the skeptical argument from hiddenness is that it basically presumes inadequacy of the evidence and begs the question from there. Schellenberg takes nonbelievers as proof positive that the evidence is not sufficient to elicit belief, but it may be that there are biases at work in the minds of unbelievers that prevent their seeing the evidence for what it is. The remedy for the latter situation is not for God to perform signs and wonders, but for unbelieving men to repent. Given the well-established

---

[32] J.L. Schellenberg, *Divine Hiddenness and Human Reason* (Ithaca, NY: Cornell University Press, 1993, 2006), p. 2.

human proclivity for dishonesty and self-deception, I would think it more likely that nonbelievers "suppress the truth in unrighteousness" (Rom. 1:18), or at least have done so at some point in the past, than that God has failed to sufficiently reveal himself.

On the other hand, hiddenness is actually a blessing to believers, for now we depend upon the power of the Holy Spirit to illuminate the truth of God and work on our behalf. Believers must apprehend God's promises by faith, inspiring hope and love that does not depend on our often faulty physical perceptions and misleading emotions. We walk by faith, not by sight (2 Cor. 5:7). Thus we are taught to rely upon the faithfulness of God and his Word. It is God's hiddenness that we emulate when we pray, fast and do good works in secret (Mat. 6:1-8).

At the same time, the invisibility of God makes all the more essential our calling to be the "light of the world" – because until either the light of God dawns on their hearts, or they face God at judgment at the end of their lives, unbelieving men have only our witness. "Knowing, therefore, the terror of the Lord, we persuade men..." (2 Cor. 5:11).

Truth

In light of the current postmodern tendencies toward cynicism, skepticism and subjectivism, Pilate's question to Christ has become more timely than ever: "What is truth?" (John 18:37). Unfortunately, these unbelieving secular attitudes have crept into the church, including the ranks of conservative-Evangelicals. Another Reformation would be in order, this time not to describe the truth but to merely recognize that there is such a thing. One of the major propositions of Scripture is that God, and his Word, are truth.

It could be said that at issue in the fall of man was the truth. God spoke the truth, Satan countered with lies, and Adam and Eve opted for the lie over the truth. Whenever God reveals himself, he reveals the truth to men. Every word of God is truth (Ps. 119). Prophets in the Old Testament were revered primarily because they spoke the truth. Accordingly, God is the truth, and the source of all truth. This would be one of a number of reasons for men to listen to God and heed his Word.

As John's Gospel makes clear, Jesus is the embodiment of truth, "the Word made flesh...full of grace and truth." Jesus is described as "the Way, the Truth, and the Life" (John 14:6), and the "Light of the world," light being a traditional symbol of truth. It is significant also that the enemy of God is "the Father of lies," since opposition to God means denial of truth.

Though it may not seem obvious at a glance, there is a deep connection between obedience and truth, for truth is more than a passing thought about life; it defines a life marked by truth. Without obedience, truth becomes an academic or philosophical interest, rather than the difference between life and death, as both Joshua in the Old Testament and James in the New Testament indicate. Without recognizing and heeding the truth, we cannot be saved in the first place (Eph. 1:13). Likewise, believers are called to abide in the truth, to stay true to what God has spoken.

Certain attributes define the truth: it is eternal (inspired of God), absolute, universal, practically essential, infinite, exclusive, doctrinal, and most importantly, centered in the person of Christ – "just as the truth is in Jesus" (Eph. 4:21). From this standpoint, doctrine is not a secondary issue, but is of primary, eternal importance.

Glory

In the Old Testament, the name "Ichabod" was famously assigned to a newborn son by a mother who had just lost her husband and father-in-law due to spiritual compromise. Appropriately enough, the name "Ichabod" means "the glory has departed" (1 Sam 4). The story in which this scene takes place is tragically ironic, contrasting the nation of Israel, comfortable and complacent in the presence of God, with a Philistine nation approaching God with dutiful reverence. This story follows after the story of Samson, another tragic tale of lost glory and failed strength. In the New Testament, likewise, men are described as "holding to a form of godliness, but denying its power" (2 Tim 3:2-5). Revelation describes churches that have fallen asleep, grown weary, and taken after material pursuits rather than the love of God. All of this is symptomatic of a generation that does not give God "the glory due to his name" (Ps 29).

As A. W. Tozer and others have remarked, the church is in desperate need of "a transforming vision of God." This starts with calling on the name of the Lord: "Show me thy glory!" (Ex 33). We in the church would do well to recall that Jesus was glorified in the same way as the Father, in the Transfiguration and in the acceptance of worship. Both John and the author of Hebrews emphasize Christ as "the glory" of the Father on earth. In performing miracles, Jesus overtly "manifested his glory" (John 2:11). Believers should similarly take heart at the glory of God as we "glory in tribulation" (Rom 5); Peter adds that we have reason to rejoice even in sufferings, anticipating the "revelation of his glory" (1 Pet 4). Finally, our eternal hope is founded on the glory of God, as our "light affliction is producing for us an eternal weight of glory far beyond all comparison" (2 Cor. 4:16-18). I should add that in a culture that positively encourages narcissism (through social media especially), meditating upon the glory of God might restore our lost sense of psychological balance. (I am reminded of the story of a psychotherapist whose suggested remedy for a deeply depressed and self-absorbed patient was to visit Niagara Falls, if only to realize that some things are larger and grander than ourselves.)

Whereas fallen man glories in himself and his own works, there is a genuine spiritual glory that can be had by men, but only as it is "subsumed" within God's glory. That is, as we work, minister, and exercise our gifts, we *reflect* the glory of God. This is as it should be, because rightly speaking we have no intrinsic glory of our own. Guthrie observes, "…God is not only assumed to be glorious, but is the pattern for the measuring of glory in others…. No glory can be greater than God's." At the same time, by partaking of God's grace we also partake of his glory: "Nevertheless, through the process of justification Paul sees the possibility of men again sharing in God's glory (Rom. 5:2)."[33]

The Trinity

The doctrine of the Trinity, the seeds of which are scattered throughout the Old Testament, was given specific prophetic expression by Isaiah: "The Virgin will be with child and will bear a son, and will call him Immanuel (Isa. 7:14, "Immanuel" meaning "God with us"). He added, "For to us a child is born…called Wonderful Counselor, Mighty God, Everlasting Father, Prince of Peace" (9:6). Isaiah's prophecy found its fulfillment in the first century AD in Bethlehem, as a child was born who would grow up to declare himself the only Son of God and confirm it through signs, deeds, and rising from the dead.

---

[33] Guthrie, p. 90.

During his time on earth, Jesus not only identified himself with God the Father, but with the "Spirit of Truth" (John 14). This Spirit would fill the disciples once Jesus had departed, would guide the disciples into all truth, and through their message would convict the world of sin, of righteousness, and of judgment (John 16:8). Through these various lines of evidence the doctrine of the Trinity emerges: the one God eternally exists as three Persons – Father, Son, and Holy Spirit.

Numerous Scriptures describe the interrelationships among the three members of the godhead. Describing Jesus, Matthew says, "He saw the Spirit of God descending like a dove... And a voice from heaven said, 'This is My Son, in whom I am well pleased'" (Matt. 3:16-17). And at the disclosure of the Great Commission, Jesus commanded the disciples to baptize "in the name of the Father and of the Son and of the Holy Spirit" (Matt. 28:19). Here each member of the Trinity is distinct, yet evidently co-equal. Indeed, the unified relationships among the Trinity are mentioned by Paul as the prime example of fellowship in the church (1 Cor. 12:4-6). Another clear indication of the triune godhead is 2 Cor. 13:4: "Now may the grace of the Lord Jesus Christ, and the love of God [i.e., the Father] and the fellowship of the Holy Spirit be with you all."

It's not so much that the Bible explicitly spells out "Trinity" as a doctrine. "Instead," argues Bird, "the Trinity is a theological inference that is drawn out of the biblical materials."[34] If it can be shown that God is one, and at the same time that Father, Son, and Holy Spirit are equally God, then we are left with the Trinity. This is how deductive reasoning works, as Sherlock Holmes famously observed: "When you have eliminated the impossible, whatever remains, however improbable, must be the truth."

In Genesis 2:24, God presents the principle of spiritual union in marriage: "the two shall become one flesh." There is to exist a unity so fundamental that it is not proper or correct to speak of either party independently of the other. The two are one in essence. So it is with the godhead. Though individually distinct (distinguishable), Father, Son and Spirit are so intertwined that they are essentially one, and it is perfectly valid for the Scriptures to declare that "The Lord God, He is One." This speaks to the theological concept of *Perichoresis*. Rhodes explains: "The

---

[34] Bird, p. 100.

doctrine of Perichoresis asserts that each member of the Godhead is fully and completely present in the person and works of the others."[35]

Paul declares plainly that "there is one God, the Father" (1Cor. 8:6). The identification of the Father with God is manifest throughout Scripture, and indeed is scarcely disputed even by cultists. So the first question to present any formidable challenges to the Trinity is the identity of the Son. The historicity of Jesus has been demonstrated with sufficient rigor for most theologians. The real question concerns the nature of his identity, specifically his Deity.

On the divinity of Christ Scripture has much to say. Jesus is specifically identified with God frequently, as in John 1:1; 20:28; Col. 2:9; Heb. 1:8; and Titus 2:13. His pre-existence is assumed (John 1:14), as in his direct role in creation (Col. 1:16; Heb. 1:2-3). He is also the judge of all men (John 5; 2 Cor. 5:10). Furthermore, numerous passages from the Old Testament have been quoted in the New Testament with the name of Jesus substituted for God (Matt. 21:15-16; Phili. 2:9-11). His titles speak of deity in Scripture: Savior, Rock, Light, Bridegroom, Alpha and Omega, I AM, King of Kings, Shepherd, Master. Thomas openly worshiped Christ as "my Lord and my God." This was not an irreverent outburst of emotion, as some have claimed, but an acknowledgment befitting the question at hand, namely whether Jesus had the power and authority to rise from the dead. In the New Testament Jesus does the works of God, has the attributes of God, and is worshiped by believers as God. His titles – God, Son of God, and Lord – all speak directly to his divinity.

Equally, the Holy Spirit is God. The very fact that his name is "Holy" attests to the Spirit's divinity, as God is described in Scripture as the only truly Holy being. Often, when God speaks, the Word says that "the Holy Spirit spoke" (Acts 28:25-27; Isa. 6:8-10). It is significant that Paul uses the terms God, Christ and Spirit interchangeably. He refers to the power of God, then of Christ, then of the Spirit (2 Cor. 4:7; 2 Cor. 12:9; Rom. 15:19). Additionally, the Spirit is clearly personal, performing personal, intelligent activities. He convicts, guides, hears, appoints (makes decisions), helps, intercedes, etc. These traits repudiate the notion that the Spirit is some "impersonal force" that God harnesses to do his will. Along with the Father and the Son, the Spirit is ascribed attributes of the Deity: eternity, omniscience, omnipotence, and omnipresence. He is involved in

---

[35] Rhodes, p. 137.

creation (Gen. 1:2), regeneration (John 3:5), inspiration of Scripture (2 Pet. 1:21), and raising from the dead (Rom. 8:11).

Again, these strands of evidence all come together to form the basis for the doctrine of the Trinity. Each member of the godhead is described as distinct, and each is identified with the only living God. The Trinity may be somewhat perplexing to consider, but the biblical data point to the unsurprising fact that God's ways and thoughts are higher than ours, and therefore not always easy to fully comprehend. If believers aren't careful we may come to intellectually disregard what the church has historically, rightly upheld as a central element of our faith. Ernest Musekiwa explains that indeed our very salvation is a function of the Trinity:

> Time after time, New Testament passages link together these three elements – Father, Son and the Spirit… The totality of God's saving presence and power can only, it would seem, be expressed by involving all three elements (for example, see 1 Corinthians 12:4-6; 2 Corinthians 1:21, 22; Ephesians 2:20-22; 2 Thessalonians 2:13-14; Titus 3:4-6; 1 Peter 1:2).[36]

My only reservation regarding the doctrine of the Trinity has to do with the perhaps overly heavy emphasis laid upon it by church leaders and theologians through the ages. My thinking is that, precisely because the doctrine is shrouded in mystery, correctly formulating it should not be the primary litmus test of orthodoxy. The doctrine of the Trinity is certainly derived from the biblical data, but the biblical data do not, in my opinion, *necessarily* require that a person profess (much less explain) the Trinity in order to be saved or right with God. Simply put, we are saved by faith in Christ. McGrath says it well:

> The doctrine of the Trinity can be regarded as the outcome of a process of sustained and critical reflection on the pattern of divine activity revealed in Scripture, and continued in Christian experience. This is not to say that Scripture contains a doctrine of the Trinity;

---

[36] Ernest Musekiwa, *Primitive Christianity as Seen in Acts* (Harare, Zimbabwe: Christian Missions Theological College and Seminary, 2014), p. 22.

rather, Scripture bears witness to a God who demands to be understood in a Trinitarian manner.[37]

Nonetheless, the Trinity does point to the unified, powerful, majestic nature of God, and learning of it does prepare evangelists and apologists for the criticisms of unbelievers who would assert that the revelation of God is "self-contradictory." Although there is much mystery and paradox in the doctrine of the Trinity, there is no contradiction.

During my time as a contributor at the Christian Cadre blog, one of the disagreements I had with a frequent atheist commenter there concerned whether there are possible worlds in which the laws of logic do not hold. I maintained that the laws of logic must hold at every possible world if the very concept of "possible worlds" is to have any meaning whatsoever. Once it is permitted that the rules of logic are not themselves necessary truths, we are left with no means to distinguish possible truths from necessary truths, let alone necessary worlds from possible worlds, nor possible worlds from impossible worlds (e.g., worlds that both exist and do not exist at the same time).

My atheist friend suggested that despite appealing to logic in many of their arguments, theists make special exceptions for theism. He then asked me this: "Do you believe that the doctrine of the Trinity is true? If you do, then how does that square with the rules of classical logic?" I believe that question to be worthy of a considered response.[38]

For clarity's sake my own reply to the first part of the question is simply "Yes." But of course what skeptics are more interested in is the second part: why Christians like me believe in the Trinity, especially when we claim to place such a high premium on the validity of logic in understanding God and the world he created.

Theologians have written volumes on the Trinity as a church dogma, as a description of divine ontology drawn from biblical statements, and as

---

[37] McGrath, p. 193-194.

[38] The remainder of this chapter is taken largely from Don McIntosh, "Is the Trinity Logically Impossible?", *Cadre Comments* [blog], <http://christiancadre.blogspot.com/2017/01/is-trinity-logically-impossible.html>.

a model of divinity that lends itself to the activity of securing human redemption. Apologists, however, are the most interested in whether or not the Trinity is actually coherent. That issue in turn concerns the logical relations among Father, Son and Spirit. According to Grudem, the set of propositions underlying the doctrine of the Trinity can be stated succinctly as follows:

1. God is three persons [*hypostases*].
2. Each person is fully God.
3. There is one God.[39]

...the problem being that these appear inconsistent. However, there are no explicit contradictions here. Additional premises would be required to create an explicit contradiction, such as

4. God is not three persons. – or –
5. Each person is less than fully God. – or –
6. There are many Gods (gods). Etc.

Clearly it would be logically problematic to say that the one God is actually three separate beings. After all, that seems to be directly translatable to 1 = 3, which is explicitly contradictory (in that something, God, is said to be both one and not-one at the same time). At issue, though, is whether the relations among the members of the godhead are absolute, or purely reflexive, identity relations. To put it another way, we need to ask ourselves, what exactly does it mean to say, "God is Father, Son and Spirit," and to also say, "Father, Son, and Spirit are God"? If it's right to say that the one God is strictly *equal* to – nothing more and nothing less – all three members of the godhead, and vice-versa, then we are saying that one equals three and effectively speaking nonsense. But I don't think it's necessarily true that the relations among the members of the godhead are purely reflexive.

---

[39] Wayne Grudem, "Trinity," *Biblical Training* (1994), <https://www.biblicaltraining.org/library/trinity-wayne-grudem>.

Some theologians have suggested these are "relative identities," identity relations that are still logically valid but in terms other than shared properties. Deutsch comments in the *Stanford Encyclopedia*:

> It is possible for objects x and y to be the same F and yet not the same G, (where F and G are predicates representing kinds of things (apples, ships, passengers) rather than merely properties of things (colors, shapes)). In such a case 'same' cannot mean absolute identity. For example, the same person might be two different passengers, since one person may be counted twice as a passenger."[40]

Now this "passenger" analogy, like most other analogies, does not apply all that well to the Trinity, but for present purposes the fact that relative identities are *possible* is enough to undercut the argument that the Trinity is explicitly, inescapably illogical.

While analogies proposed for the Trinity are typically imperfect (as analogies are generally), they do often serve to underscore that the Trinity is a mystery in need of further investigation rather than an example of explicit illogic. According to Louis Markos, echoing Dorothy Sayers, the Trinity is analogous to a work of art (such as a book), consisting *simultaneously* of Idea, Energy, and Power:

> The Idea (which she also calls the Book as Thought) is the invisible conception of the entire work that resides outside of time and space in the mind of the artist. The Energy (the Book as Written) takes the invisible Idea and embodies it in the material, space/time reality of our world; it proceeds from the Idea while still being one with it. The Power (the Book as Read) proceeds from both the Idea and Energy; it allows a reader to experience the Idea through its embodiment and the artist to really *see* his work.[41]

---

[40] Harry Deutsch, "Relative Identity," *Stanford Encyclopedia of Philosophy* (2007), <https://plato.stanford.edu/entries/identity-relative/>.

[41] Louis Markos, *Apologetics for the Twenty-first Century* (Wheaton, IL: Crossway, 2010), p. 94.

Various Trinitarian allusions are evident here: the metaphysical transcendence of the Idea (i.e., the Father); the physical instantiation of the Energy (the Son), and the empowering and illumination provided by the Power (the Holy Spirit), proceeding from both the Idea and the Energy. So there are three instantiations of the one Book.

Here again the analogy appears imperfect. (If the Book itself analogizes the godhead, and a book is written by an author, who is the author in all this? Clearly an ontological distinction should be made between the artist and his work.) Quite apart from whether God truly exists as the Trinity, however, it should surprise no one that there are few readily applicable worldly analogies for the ultimate spiritual reality. And skeptics familiar with scientific theories should know that nature houses numerous mysteries of its own: how an entropic universe can come into existence unaided; how quantum mechanics can be reconciled with general relativity; how chemical evolution can take place apart from replicators that only operate within living systems, etc. Meanwhile some serious Trinitarian models[42] purport to provide solutions – or at least potential solutions – beyond merely pointing out that the Trinity is not formally contradictory.

---

[42] Michael Rea suggests that "there are two main strategies for solving the problem: the Relative Identity (RI) strategy, and the Social Trinitarian (ST) strategy;" and further suggests the RI models to be much more effective. -- "Relative Identity and the Doctrine of the Trinity," *Philosophia Christi*, 5, 2 (2003), p. 431.

3. Christology: Son of God and Son of Man

"When the fullness of the time had come, God sent forth his Son..." So says Paul in Galatians 4:4, in arguing the supremacy of faith in Christ over the works of the law. When Paul spoke these words, the first century world was lost in spiritual darkness. The gods of the Roman and Greek pantheons had no reality, hence no power, to guide men or keep them humble or honest or just. Meanwhile, the old priesthood guarding the law and the covenant of God had degenerated to such a point that the priests could scarcely be distinguished from the pagans around them. Just then, as Paul says, the Son of God came into the world and changed the destiny of God's people forever. Clearly the study of Christology, of the Person and work of Jesus Christ, is essential to any Christian who wants to understand theology and to any non-Christian who wants to understand Christianity.

The Word Made Flesh

John declared in his Gospel, "In the beginning was the Word, and the Word was with God, and the Word was God" (John 1:1). As the eternal creator of all things, God exists eternally. God exists outside the limitations of the "space-time continuum" and thus has the power to create it. Eternity on this view is not merely an endless stretch of time, but is another *dimension* independent of time. So "all things were made though Him" (John 1:3). John says further in his first epistle, "That which was from the beginning [God] .... The life was manifested, and we have seen it" (1 John 1:1, 2). By proclaiming Christ as the eternal God manifested in the flesh, John repudiated the ancient Docetic heresy, which held that because matter is evil, a good God could not dwell in a physical body.

As it turns out, Docetism never completely went away. In recent decades, in fact, the very existence of Jesus Christ, a man who clearly lived and died in first century Judea (i.e., the "historical Jesus") has somehow become controversial. Facing arguments from a handful of misguided but highly influential mythicists (mainly on the Internet), Christian believers today, like apostles of Jesus in the first century, are called upon to defend the truth "that Jesus Christ has come in the flesh" (1 John 4:2-3). Stephen

J. Bedard, one such Christian, argues that strong consensus among scholars amounts to *prima facie* justification for accepting the Jesus of history:

> There is a strong scholarly consensus that Jesus existed. This is not just with evangelical Christians, but with liberal Christians, Jews, Muslims, agnostics and atheists. They may disagree about Jesus' identity and whether he performed miracles, but his existence is not an issue."[43]

This is not to say that truth is a function of majority opinion, but it does suggest that mythicists bear a heavy burden of proof: "It is possible that the entire scholarly world except for two or three PhDs is wrong. But it is worth asking why this consensus is so strong."[44] Given that mythicists have not in fact met their burden of proof, as most mythicists themselves would acknowledge, there is little need for me to address the issue further in order to proceed with Christology.

Another obstacle to a Christian understanding of Jesus, however, and almost as intellectually irresponsible as mythicism, is the presumed dilemma between "the Jesus of history" and "the Christ of faith." It is a sad commentary on both the intellectual state of modern academia and the spiritual state of the church that, as Guthrie says, "Anyone who attempts to assess the place of Jesus Christ within NT theology must first make clear his position relative to the modern debate over the Christ of faith and the historical Jesus"[45] – as if the two were mutually exclusive. This dichotomy is basically a restatement of the Enlightenment critic Gotthold Lessing's famous "ugly ditch" between historical events and eternal truths. According to certain exceedingly critical contemporary scholars, Lessing's ditch simply cannot be crossed. To the contrary, contend Bock and Wallace,

---

[43] Stephen J. Bedard, *Unmasking the Jesus Myth* (St. Catherines, Ontario, Canada: Hope's Reason Ministries, 2016), p. 9.

[44] Bedard, p. 9.

[45] Guthrie, p. 219.

Lessing's ditch is not impassible. Points of contact between Jesus and his followers in terms of their core message reveal agreement that Jesus came and died, that he was raised by God in an act of unique vindication, and that he functioned in a role that completed God's promise and allows him to bear the name Christ.[46]

Probably in conscious awareness of Gnostic and Docetic influences, John explicitly affirms not only the physical reality of Christ's Incarnation, but his eternal pre-existence as the *Logos* (a Greek term most often translated as "word"). Incarnation is the unification of human nature with the eternal Logos. The divine took on human form and nature in the womb of Mary, and began the "process" of Incarnation, in which the entire Trinitarian godhead was involved.

That is, the Father sent the Son to be "born of a woman" (Gal. 4:4); the Son "dwelt among us" (John 1:14); and the Spirit overshadowed Mary so that she would bear the Son of God (Matt. 1:18). The Logos thus did partake of flesh and blood, and came in the likeness of sinful flesh (Phil. 2:7; Rom. 8:3). According to McGrath, recounting the view of the second century apologist Justin Martyr, "The Logos…is known by both Christian and pagan philosophers; the latter, however, have only partial access to it, whereas Christians have full access to it, on account of its manifestation in Christ."[47]

By way of the Logos concept, Justin was able to bridge the divide between Christian and pagan understandings of God, and make his appeal to find the fullness of knowledge literally *embodied* in Christ. At the same time he repudiated popular Gnostic and Docetic teachings that God could not inhabit a physical body. Justin and the early apologists knew full well that the gospel entails God dwelling in human flesh, not merely in appearance but in reality.

So later in his Gospel, John records an exchange between Jesus and his critics, in which Jesus states, "Before Abraham was born, I AM." This

---

[46] Darrell L. Bock & Daniel B. Wallace, *Dethroning Jesus: Exposing Popular Culture's Quest to Unseat the Biblical Christ* (Nashville: Thomas Nelson, 2007), p. 29.

[47] McGrath, p. 356-357.

was such a strong declaration of Deity, not only because of the reference to pre-existence, but because it matched God's response to Moses' question as to his identity: "I AM WHO I AM." Colossians says that Christ is "before all things" (1:17). And when John says, "He was in the beginning with God," he alludes to the eternal fellowship of the members of the godhead, as indicated in Genesis 1 ("let us create man in our image"). So Christ is God, but does not constitute the entire godhead. With him are the Father and the Spirit, all three being truly the One God Almighty. In the Incarnation the Son of God "emptied himself," not of his divine attributes or power, but of his right and prestige as God Almighty. Jesus clearly displayed the attributes of deity: He performed miracles, or "signs" as John stated. He was omnipresent, in heaven even as in the world (John 3:13). He was (and is!) immutable, the same "yesterday, today and forever" (Heb. 13:8). What he gave up was his glory, often deferring to the Father (John 5:20), and his eternal joys and riches in heaven (2 Cor. 8:9).

Suffering Servant and Triumphant King

Under the Old Covenant, Israel had to sacrifice to find favor with God. Representing the nation were the priests, the Levites, who had to enter into the presence with great trepidation. By contrast, Jesus has offered up a more perfect sacrifice, himself, taking on the role of both the priest and the sacrifice – both of them perfect, without blemish. By faith, believers rest in the knowledge that all sacrifices for sin have been forever consummated in the sacrifice of Christ. He is the "Branch," the messianic seed of David, the Son of Man, the suffering Servant (Isa. 4:2; Zech. 3:8; 6:12).

Prophetic pictures of Christ also indicate his pre-existence. He was the lamb slain before the foundation of the world, promised and portrayed at the fall (Gen. 3) and the Passover (Ex. 12), now actively redeeming men by his blood (1 Pet. 2:24; John 1:29). As the Servant of God, Jesus fulfills prophecies from Exodus 21 and especially Isaiah 42-53. Isaiah describes the Servant of God, Messiah, in glorious detail, so that no one could rightly dispute the connection with Christ. This Servant was to be, and now is, anointed of the Spirit of God, through which Jesus speaks wisdom (Isa. 11:2), heals and restores (Luke 4:18), and lives in power and holiness

(Rom. 1:4). Isaiah prophesied that Messiah "would not cry out." In refusing to cower or cave in before the temptations of Satan to declare himself king over the Roman Empire, or to perform miracles for Herod or the Pharisees on demand, Jesus fulfilled the role of Messiah as a ruler equal in humility and power.

Christ's humility was and is demonstrated by his gentleness with the weak. Jesus refused to judge those who were already broken or repentant. Thus he was stern with the self-righteous Pharisees, but kind and compassionate to the infirm and poor in spirit (John 8:1-10; Matt. 5:3). Whereas Isaiah said that Messiah would "bring forth justice for truth," Jesus embodied the truth (John 14:6), and equally resisted and condemned lies (John 8:44). This means that when the dominion of Jesus is complete, there will be no place for atheism, false religions or unbelief. So along with humility, Jesus will exercise judgment. "The coastlands shall wait for his law," said Isaiah, and Jesus, who has fulfilled the law in letter and spirit, will one day set all things in order by righteous judgment.

The Servant's mission is first to do the will of the Father (John 17:4). That will consisted of humiliation, suffering and exaltation, i.e., both cross and crown (1 Pet. 1:11). Though he was rejected by many, including his own, Jesus will prevail and bring in a final harvest of both Jew and Gentile. The Servant speaks graciously, comforting and uplifting the weary and distraught (Matt. 11:28; Mark 2:5). He is humble, willing to learn and obey authorities, endure insults and slander, and at last face the humiliation of the cross. He is willing to suffer for the sake of his Father's will and his love for people (Heb. 2:10). As a Servant, Christ embraced the lowest station in life, rejected pomp and splendor, and experienced the worst kinds of wounds. Nonetheless, he suffered patiently and was at last rewarded in the presence of the Father.

Having triumphed over his enemies and having defeated death itself, Jesus is now not merely Servant but King, as signified in the Old Testament repeatedly. As King of Israel, Jesus held fast to the dictates of the law, and moreover fulfilled it in spirit (Matt. 5:17). He preached that the kingdom of God had actually arrived in his person (Matt. 4:17; Mark 1:15). The New Testament elsewhere describes Jesus as "King of the saints" (Rev. 15:3) and the "King of peace" (Heb. 7:1-3). This peace comes through righteousness. Jesus loves righteousness, fulfills righteousness, judges with righteousness, and has become our righteousness. He is King of heaven (Rev. 19:12; Dan. 7:18) and King of kings (Rev. 19:16).

As the "King of glory" (Ps. 24), Jesus reigns in triumph, having overcome temptation, humiliation, abuse, and finally execution. Death itself could not defeat the sinless Son of God. Accordingly, when Jesus returns he will not appear lowly and riding a donkey, but coming in the clouds in glory as conquering King.

Son of God and Son of Man

Jesus is the beloved Son. He is "functionally subordinate" to the Father in that he does the Father's will, yet remains ontologically equal to the Father as a full-fledged member of the triune godhead. He has been with the Father, and has been loved of the Father, from the beginning (John 1:18, 24). He is the Son born unto us, yet his name is Mighty God, Everlasting Father and Wonderful Counselor, i.e., the eternal Deity (Isa. 9:6). The Son acts on behalf of both God and men, to secure redemption. Jesus is the I AM, the bread of life, the light of the world, the door of salvation, the resurrection and the life, the way, the truth and the life, and the vine (John 8:58; 8:12; 10:7; 11:25; 14:6; 15:1). He is the eternal God who has visited and befriended us as a man.

Jesus was worshiped as God by the cleansed leper (Matt. 8:2), Jairus the synagogue ruler (Matt. 9:18), the disciples in the boat and at the Great Commission (Matt. 14:33; 28:9), the woman in Canaan with the demonized daughter (Matt. 15:22), and the wife of Zebedee (Matt. 20:20). Appropriately, then, he exhibited the attributes and moral character of God himself. He was righteous (Acts 22:14), he was truth (John 1:14), and he was holy and pure (Acts 4:27). Equally, Jesus possesses the theological attributes of the Deity. He is omnipresent (Mt. 18:20), omniscient (John 2:24-25; John 1:48), omnipotent (Phil. 3:20; Rev. 1:18), and immutable (Heb. 13:8). He does the works of God: creation (John 1:3), providence (Heb. 1:3; Col. 1:17), miracles, resurrections and final judgment (Acts 17:31; Rev. 20:13). Jesus also forgives sins, so that the Pharisees rightly associated Jesus' claim to forgive the sins of others as a self-assertion of deity. According to Guthrie, "Jesus as Son makes the claim to be the exclusive revelation of the Father. He alone has seen the Father... He therefore is the sole medium by which men may come to know him."[48]

---

[48] Guthrie, p. 315.

Through the centuries theologians have wrestled with the doctrine of the Incarnation, the "mystery of godliness" that God was manifest in the flesh. These efforts eventually yielded a coherent theology with the support of a consensus of scholars, but along the way turned up numerous questionable doctrines and outright heresies.[49] The resolution to these conflicts was found in the formulation of Chalcedon, a theological statement to the effect that Jesus is a single personality exhibiting both natures. Jesus is both Son of God and Son of Man. In his person transcendence and immanence meet. Being the Son of God, Jesus literally embodied the "fullness of the godhead."

But Jesus is also the Son of Man. In fact Jesus most often referred to himself as "Son of Man" while on earth. A title taken from Daniel 7, "Son of Man" signifies a number of important messianic truths. These include Christ's *authority, humiliation, suffering* and *death*. On one hand, speaking as Son of Man, Jesus has the authority to forgive sins and heal diseases (Mark 2:9-11), and assert that he is "Lord of the Sabbath" (Mark 2:28). But being a man, Jesus was subject to suffering and death for our sins. At the same time, bearing the authority of God himself, he could not be *held* by death. "As Son of Man," says Guthrie, "Jesus knew he would not be exempt from death, but he knew also that he would triumph over it in resurrection."[50]

As we Evangelicals often say, Jesus was, and is, "100% God and 100% man." God in Christ has taken on human nature, and will ever be the God-Man, Jesus Christ. Historians and theologians have framed this rather intricate relationship of the two natures in terms of "hypostatic union." The basic idea is that Christ is not the sum of two natures, but the divine person. Bird explains: "What the doctrine of the hypostatic union teaches is that these two natures are united in one person in the God-man Jesus. He is not two persons; he is one.[51] Jesus did things that only a biological creature can do, such as experience hunger, thirst, and death; and

---

[49] See Chapter Nine, "Theology Beyond the Fringes: Heresies in History," for a comprehensive examination of heresy in the church.

[50] Guthrie, p. 281.

[51] Bird, p. 484.

things only God can do, such as foresee the future, read the thoughts and motives of men, work miracles and rise from the dead.

The hypostatic union was not the consequence of a church council but of a divine mission to salvage mankind. This was accomplished through the humiliation of Christ, by God condescending to take on human flesh and the meekness of a servant (Phil. 2:6-8). His humiliation began at birth, in the little village of Bethlehem. It continued as Jesus took the difficult route of learning, growing, and developing as a man among other men. Jesus learned to read, and astonished his peers with great wisdom (Luke 2:46, 47). He was nurtured by his mother, and was subjected to the authority of his parents (Luke 2:51). He "grew in favor with God and men," meaning that he acquired wisdom along with social skills. He experienced all the challenges, weaknesses and infirmities of human nature, yet resisted every temptation to sin. He hungered, thirsted, slept, and wept. Thus the God of all wisdom says, "I am troubled;" the omnipotent Creator of the universe falls asleep for lack of rest, and the Giver of the water of life thirsts. These are not contradictions, but evidences of the hypostatic union in the God-Man.

Promised Messiah

Christ's Incarnation was no accident, but was undertaken for specific purposes. By becoming a man the divine Logos confirmed the promises made to the fathers (Rom. 15:8-12). Wherever the Old Testament speaks of Messiah, the New speaks of fulfillment. All the types, symbols, rites and ceremonies foreshadowing Christ have at last been fulfilled. "Jesus is the Messiah because he is the one prophesied about in the Old Testament. The claim that Jesus' preaching was foretold in the Old Testament was a basic element of apostolic preaching."[52]

Additionally, Jesus came that the Gentiles might partake of the promises and the mercies of God (Rom. 15:9). Throughout the OT, allusions are made of blessings for the Gentiles. The promises of enjoying Messiah's rule, of salvation, of the outpouring of the Spirit (Isa. 54; Hos. 1:10; Joel 2:28-29) have been revealed and fulfilled in Christ. He has come, moreover, to "put away sin" by the offering of himself in its place (1 John

---

[52] Bird, p. 359.

3:5). Whereas the old sacrificial system could only temporarily cover sin, the Incarnation of Christ permitted God to provide a pure and permanent sacrifice, superior to all others (Heb. 9, 10).

By the same principle, Jesus is now a faithful and sympathetic High Priest, one who has suffered temptation but overcome (Heb. 4:15). Jesus endured manifold temptations, from the wilderness to the cross, and in so doing proved himself qualified to be our Messiah. Jesus came also to reveal the Father to us (John 14:7-11). Thus, as the Christ, he shows us the Father's love, care and concern, and beneficence toward us all. Jesus has come to destroy the works of the devil (1 John 3:8), including the works of the flesh (Gal. 5:19). Finally, Jesus came to give us an example to follow (1 Pet. 2:21). He called poor and weary men to learn from him (Matt. 11:29). He was holy, meek and lowly, humble, and steadfastly obedient to the will of the Father. He was stellar in compassion, purity of motives, prayer, and of course the faithful endurance on the cross, borne of love for mankind.

Though a stumbling block to intellectuals, the Virgin Birth makes perfect sense in light of Christology, as the means by which a sinless divine nature could come to inhabit earthly flesh. Anselm argued that God merely bypassed the usual human agency of generation and impregnation by forming Christ directly in the womb. Regardless of how "improbable" the Virgin Birth may appear in a scientific age (as if omnipotence were bound by probabilities!), the doctrine is confirmed by a number of statements (Phil. 2:7; John 1:14; Gal. 4:4; Heb. 2:14; Gen, 3:15; Luke 1:35; Heb. 10:5). The Father "prepared" a body for the Son, one which has not partaken of the sin nature inherent in human flesh and blood. It was thoroughly physical, thoroughly human, yet untainted by the effects of the fall. This makes the Virgin Birth essential, and a *bona fide* miracle. It should be pointed out that God did not fertilize the egg of Mary and impregnate her; rather, God created Jesus in the womb. He would be conceived by a miracle, but born as humanity. Equally, it is important to realize that Mary did not "pass on" her own sinful nature to Jesus, any more than did Joseph. She merely served as the *vessel* through which Christ would enter the human race.

The Virgin Birth is furthermore no theological invention of the Gospel writers, but was prophesied in Isaiah 7:14, a promise that clearly extended beyond the immediate historical context: "Therefore the Lord Himself will give you a sign: Behold, the virgin shall conceive and bear a

Son, and shall call His name Immanuel ["God-With-Us"]." Now this has proven a controversial text, as many scholars have noted that "virgin" here (*'almâ* in Hebrew) best translates to "young woman." But other scholars[53] point out that in Scripture a *sign* is most often some sort of miracle, all the more so when God himself is the one offering to show it. And on the face of it there is nothing especially significant about young women conceiving and having children. Thus whereas Jesus is the Son of David, he is also the promised "seed of the woman." (This may help further explain the apparent disparity between the genealogies of Matthew and Luke. It appears that Joseph descended from Solomon and Mary from Nathan, both descendants of David.) By coming to earth as a sinless man born of a woman, Jesus took on the role of Mediator for the sake of humanity, to bridge the gulf between man and God and rescue mankind from the grips of darkness. Paul called this the "ministry of reconciliation" between men and God.

Jesus was baptized, not by a ranking priest but by John the Baptist, a "layman" minister. Yet John was a prophet, the greatest of prophets (Matt. 11:13). Baptism was evidently part of John's calling to "prepare the way of the Lord" (Isa. 4:3; Mark 1:2). As a devout and pious believer, John was reluctant to baptize Jesus, fearing it might suggest a reversal of their respective spiritual roles (Matt. 3:13). However, Jesus was not getting baptized as an act of repentance, but as a priest entering the ministry "to fulfill all righteousness" (Matt. 3:15). He was doing things the way they are supposed to be done. This act of baptism by water also foreshadowed the terrible baptism of suffering and death Jesus would willingly undergo for humanity as the Son of God.

The Spirit drove Jesus into the wilderness not to find out whether or not Jesus was faithful, but to prove that Jesus was faithful indeed. Some say that Jesus was able to sin, and did not, whereas others say that Jesus was strictly unable to sin. An argument for the latter position could be made on the grounds that Jesus is not merely a "second Adam," but the only God-Man, and therefore lives above the temptations brought on by sinful flesh. The temptation was real, however, in the sense that Jesus was tempted to break under the strain of human weakness, and therefore tempted to break his dedicated fast, but he was never tempted to sin against

---

[53] See for example Charles L. Feinberg, "The Virgin Birth and Isaiah 7:14," *Master's Seminary Journal* (Spring 2011).

the holiness of God. In the end he stood on the Word of God and thereby stood down the very real temptation to compromise his mission.

Substitutionary Sacrifice

One question that historians and theologians still cannot answer definitively is, "Who crucified Jesus Christ?" Pilate delivered Jesus to his fate, but only at the insistence of the mob, who would not listen to reason but only shouted louder for his crucifixion. In turn, the people acted at the deliberate instigation of the chief priests. Pilate buckled under the pressure, washed his hands of the matter, and assigned the act of carrying out the sentence to Roman soldiers. In addition to these historical factors a more disturbing theological factor is at work, namely the sin of mankind, for which Jesus laid down his life. In a very real sense my own sins have nailed Jesus Christ to a cross of torture (Acts 2:23).

Let it not be said that Jesus was a hapless victim of violence. He willingly laid down his life (John 10:17). As the Lamb of God, Jesus knew his mission and complied fully with the will of the Father. Jesus was ever aware of his fate, and spoke frequently of the cross to his disciples. He also knew the necessity of his death for the salvation of mankind. Whereas the law can only condemn transgression, Jesus came to fulfill the law's demands on behalf of humanity. This was the ultimate act of grace, which had been prefigured in the Old Testament: in the covering of Adam and Eve with animal skins in the Garden, Abel's offering of a lamb for sin, the sacrifice of Isaac, the Passover in Egypt, the Levitical sacrificial system, and the brazen serpent in the wilderness. Jesus was offered "through the eternal Spirit" without spot to God (Heb. 9:14), and it pleased the Father to see the labor of his soul (Isa 52). So the entire Trinitarian godhead was complicit in the crucifixion.

Jesus tasted death for every man (Heb. 2:9). Behind this was a fourfold purpose: atonement, reconciliation, redemption, and substitution. Atonement means covering and cleansing from sin. In the OT sacrifices had to be repeated and applied to given transgressions. Reconciliation means reuniting God and man, restoring the breach that had been opened through sin. Redemption involves the issues of cost and payment for sin (Eph. 1:7). Apart from Christ, men are slaves, "sold under sin" (Rom. 7:14). But as slaves on the market, we have been bought by Christ and liberated. In the process we have been freed from the emptiness of iniquity and the curse of the law.

There have been many "theories of atonement." Michael Bird includes among these: *recapitulation* ("reversing" the effects of sin); *ransom* (from the rightful jurisdiction of the devil); the "Christus Victor" model of victory in spiritual battle; *satisfaction* of God's demand for payment of sin; a humanistic-leaning *moral influence* theory; and finally, the theory of *penal substitution*. While most of these theories have some scriptural merit, my view is that penal substitution probably best encapsulates the message of the New Testament.[54]

As a substitute offered in our place, Christ died for the sins of others, not his own – because he has committed none. The Father laid on him the iniquity of us all (Isa. 53:6). In the same way that Adam's sin was imputed to us, the righteousness of Christ has been imputed to us. His substitutionary sacrifice is available and efficacious for all who will believe (John 3:16; 1 Tim. 2:6; Titus 2:11). Salvation further depends not only on what Jesus Christ has done, but *who he is*. For this reason theologians like Alister McGrath maintain that Christology and soteriology should be studied together as a single domain of Christian theology: "Christology and soteriology are…two sides of the same coin, rather than two independent areas of thought."[55]

Risen Savior

The resurrection ensures the efficacy and finality of Christ's atonement. Resurrection means the acceptance by the Father of the perfect sacrifice by the Son. And by our identification with the Son, it means eternal life for believers. It also fulfills a spiritual law: that the one who does not sin will live forever. Without the resurrection, on the other hand, our faith is in vain (1 Cor. 15:14). A resurrection-less gospel would leave us with no objective basis for the hope of eternal life. This would mean further that all in history who have believed have done so for nothing. It

---

[54] It should be noted that Bird himself offers some powerful arguments for the Christus Victor view; see *Evangelical Theology*, pp. 410-420.

[55] McGrath, p. 346.

would mean that Christians are living a lie, at most a compelling fiction, and doing so often at the cost of their own lives. It would mean that the apostles were shameless liars (1 Cor. 15:15-19).

Yet the resurrection is true. The resurrection is not only historically well attested but predicted clearly in the Old Testament. David said to God, "Thou wilt not...suffer thy Holy One to see corruption" (Ps. 16:10; Acts 2:25-27). Isaiah noted that despite the sacrifice of his Servant, the Lord would "prolong his days" (Isa. 53:9-12). Yet more clearly, Jesus explicitly spoke of his own resurrection repeatedly (Mt. 16:21; 17:19; 20:18, 19; Luke 9:22; John 2:18-22).

Historical evidence for the resurrection begins with the empty tomb, but also includes the testimony of the women at the tomb, the widely reported post-resurrection appearances of Christ to the apostles, and the birth of the early church in Jerusalem, the very site of Christ's crucifixion, and finally, the conversion of Saul of Tarsus. William Lane Craig has successfully defended the resurrection using a "minimal facts" approach based on four basic historical observations:

- Jesus' burial
- the discovery of his empty tomb
- his post-mortem appearances
- the origin of the disciples' belief in his resurrection[56]

Christ's resurrection confirms the existence of God, the power of God, the Deity of Christ, and again, the assurance of our *own* resurrection at the last day. Christ is the firstfruits of a church-wide resurrection (1 Cor. 15:20-23). I would be remiss not to mention here that according to Scripture one day *all* will rise, believers and nonbelievers alike, whether to everlasting life or everlasting torment.

Following his resurrection Jesus likely ascended twice to heaven. The first ascension occurred shortly after the resurrection, when Jesus was transported into the presence of the Father. For this reason he told Mary, "Do not cling to Me, for I have not ascended to My Father." Following

---

[56] See "Is There Historical Evidence for the Resurrection of Jesus? The Craig-Ehrman Debate," *Reasonable Faith*, March 2006, <https://www.reasonablefaith.org/media/debates/is-there-historical-evidence-for-the-resurrection-of-jesus-the-craig-ehrman/>.

this first ascension he returned to encourage and instruct the disciples, and impart to them the Great Commission. After forty days of this ministry to his own, Jesus was "received up out of their sight" (Acts 1:9).

As the book of Hebrews notes repeatedly, Jesus is now seated at the right hand of the Father. He reserves the right to this majesty, as the heir of all things, the creator of the worlds, the brightness of God's glory, the image of God, the upholder of all things, and the one who sacrificed himself for our sins. Now Jesus enjoys preeminence with the Father, retaining ultimate authority (Matt. 28:18), giving gifts to the church (Eph. 4:7-11), interceding for the saints (Heb. 7:25), serving as an advocate for us to the Father (1 John 2:1-2), preparing us as a bride for eternal life in his presence (John 14:1-3; Eph. 5:25-27). Jesus is our everything.

4. Soteriology: Many Called, Few Chosen

Despite great scientific advances in recent years, great mysteries of the universe remain. One of these mysteries concerns what the famed astrophysicist Stephen Hawking once termed the "unification of physics." In *A Brief History of Time*, Hawking described back in 1988 what still amounts to the Holy Grail of theoretical science – a unified theory of physics: "Today scientists describe the universe in terms of two basic theories – the general theory of relativity and quantum mechanics.... One of the major endeavors in physics today... is the search for a new theory that incorporates them both – a quantum theory of gravity."[57] While the search since then has apparently turned up little in terms of consistent, satisfactory results, the unification of physics remains a subject worthy of our consideration. As Hawking concludes, "A complete, consistent, unified theory is only the first step: our goal is a complete understanding of the events around us, and of our own existence."[58]

Something similar could be said of our understanding of salvation in Scripture. To understand biblical *soteriology* (the study of the doctrine of salvation) is to see the big picture – to get a glimpse of our place as morally responsible human beings in the plan of an all-powerful God as a clue to the meaning of the events that make up our everyday existence. And there is no better sourcebook for viewing the big picture than Paul's letter to the Romans.

The book of Romans may be seen as a unification of individual theological essentials: of universal sin, blood atonement, grace without measure, salvation by faith, renewed relationship with God, freedom from bondage under the law, and finally, an eschatological vision of the higher purpose of God as revealed in human history. This last revelation, the subject of chapters 9-11, is often bypassed by Bible teachers because it involves seemingly irreconcilable concepts such as the sovereignty of God

---

[57] Stephen Hawking, *A Brief History of Time* (New York: Bantam Books, 1996), p. 12. (Originally published 1988.)

[58] Hawking, p. 171.

and individual human responsibility. (As a former pastor of mine confessed in a sermon: "That is a theological pretzel I'm not even going to attempt to unravel.") Perhaps these teachers could learn something from their counterparts in the secular sciences: The fact that the big picture extends somewhat beyond the scope of human understanding is no reason to cease exploring it altogether. Indeed, that fact is precisely what makes the picture in the book of Romans so big. This examination of soteriological issues of calling, election and faith will therefore be largely based on the book of Romans, especially chapters 9 through 11.

Like any other portion of Scripture, Romans 9-11 is best understood in its various contexts. The particular historical context of Romans reveals that Paul is concerned with mending a widening breach between a growing contingent of Gentiles and a Jewish minority making up a threatened if not openly persecuted church community. The Roman historian Suetonius' record of the expulsion of the Jews from Rome by Claudius in A.D. 49 indicates that the Jews particularly had felt the heat of persecution and likely had lost their majority position in the church.[59]

Evidence from Acts 15 and the letters to the Galatians and Corinthians suggest that the Jewish and Gentile factions in the church misunderstood and mistrusted one another. Paul is concerned with healing the breach, addressing both parties alternatively throughout his letter with assurances of spiritual equality (2:11; 3:9-24; 3:29) and appeals to mutual respect (14-15). Paul's main thesis is a gospel message "to the Jew first and also to the Greek" (1:16). The historical situation thus explains Paul's division of humanity in the salvation scheme of Rom. 9-11 into the nation of Israel and the Gentile nations.

Moreover, Romans is marked by an insistent, almost apologetic demonstration of God's righteousness – as revealed in the preceding chapters (1-8), first through his righteous judgment of all men as sinners and then in his righteous redemption of men by the propitiatory sacrifice of Christ on the cross. In chapters 9 through 11, Paul extends this theme to apply to entire nations and peoples as yet another striking testimony to God's sovereign grace, wisdom and righteousness. Most importantly, Romans is about the gospel of our salvation. Paul's message is not a dry

---

[59] See F.F. Bruce, "Christianity Under Claudius," *Bulletin of the John Rylands Library*, 44 (March 1962), p. 318.

academic treatise but a joyful declaration of good news, evidenced in 9-11 by the salvation of both Jews and Gentiles in fulfillment of the purpose of God in the earth.

The Unassailable Sovereignty of God

Chapter Nine opens with the disclosure of Paul's burden for the Jews, "my countrymen according to the flesh," who for the most part had failed to embrace Jesus as the Messiah (v.1-5). Paul's anguish not only demolishes any imagined theological basis for anti-Semitism in the church, but raises the profound question: How is it that God's "chosen people" have seemingly not been chosen? Paul assures us that "the word of God has not failed" (v.6), and supplies a twofold response: First he reminds readers that "Israel" pertains to more than the physical ancestry of Abraham, but rather to the community of elect believers throughout history chosen by God and defined by his promise. So even among Israelites salvation begins with divine election and initiative. Moreover, salvation is a purpose fulfilled strictly by God's grace, irrespective of human works. It is a principle vividly expressed by God himself in the Old Testament: "Jacob I have loved but Esau I have hated." Jacob had few redeeming qualities, yet God chose him.

Now when we hear of God "choosing" people, many of us think right away of God electing certain individuals for salvation. But there are certainly other possibilities. One such possibility is that the choice in question concerns which individuals are used to transmit the hope of salvation, not which individuals are eternally saved as a result. Leighton Flowers cautions against jumping to conclusions: "When approaching the Scripture one must seek to discern what kind of divine choice is being referenced, without merely assuming every choice of God is about individuals being elected unto effectual salvation."[60]

God's sovereign decisions serve to confound human pride and demonstrate the centrality of God's grace in the plan of salvation. The fact that we have been "predestined" – whatever that means, exactly – indicates that our salvation is "to the praise of His glory" (Eph. 1:12). But this all leads to further questions, seemingly logical from a human viewpoint: "Is

---

[60] Leighton Flowers, *The Potter's Promise: A Biblical Defense of Traditional Soteriology* (Evansville, IN: Trinity Academic Press, 2017), p. 106.

there unrighteousness with God?" (v.14) Is it really necessary to "hate" (reject) Esau in order to "love" (receive) Jacob? Paul is undaunted by such questions. He answers by appealing firstly to the sovereignty of God himself, indicated in his words to Moses in verse 15: "I will have mercy on whomever I will... and I will have compassion on whomever I will..." Paul's answer reveals the reality of a divine perspective and prerogative, which really should surprise no one. It's only to be expected that the omnipotent Creator would have a different perspective than does his creation. God is sovereign, and if he wasn't sovereign he wouldn't be God.

On the other hand, Paul's focus is not merely on God's sovereignty but his mercy. The call to salvation is "not of him who wills nor of him who runs but of God who shows mercy" (v.16). It cannot be attained by willpower or works. It is an act of pure mercy because, as Paul established earlier in chapters 1-3, all men are deserving of judgment as sinners. So would there be unrighteousness in God granting mercy to certain of these sinners? No, because extending undeserved kindness is not unrighteous. Grace is a gift. Consequently, God is under no obligation to save Pharaoh (or anyone else) even while saving his own elect from under Pharaoh's cruel dominion.

To the contrary, God uses Pharaoh for his own larger redemptive purposes – in much the same way that Pharaoh has exploited God's people for his own sinful purposes for so many years. In the process of all this, Pharaoh becomes hardened. A frightful spiritual dichotomy thus emerges, as it appears that there are but two kinds of people: those finding mercy and those hardened. "He has mercy on whom he wills and whom he wills he hardens" (v.18).

Hence the next question to appear in Paul's rhetorical dialogue has to do with an objection against what is essentially a fatalistic doctrine of predestination: "Why does he still find fault? For who has resisted his will?" (v.19). Why blame Esau if God hated him, or Pharaoh if God hardened him? Paul at this point subtly inserts human responsibility into the whole equation for the first time (and certainly not for the last). He answers a paradoxical question with another: "[W]ho are you to reply against God?" Or to put it another way, "How can you ask this, since replying against God this way shows you capable of resisting his will?" One cannot be truly subject to God's irresistible sovereignty, as commonly understood, and argue against it at the same time. Objecting to God's sovereign rule reveals not only the folly of the will, but its power. The often overlooked fact borne out by this text is that men can indeed reply against God – and they do so routinely.

But the fatalistic interpretation is faulty for a few other reasons. First, the context of Rom. 9-11 has to do with God's utilizing of individual lives in history as parts of his larger preordained plan of salvation; it really has nothing to say on whether those individuals are, or are not, or can ever be, saved or free to choose or anything else. Robert Shank thus rebuts the claim that Romans is a Calvinistic treatise, "Many have failed to recognize that Paul's consideration in Rom. 9:6-29 is the question of the circumstance of Israel, rather than the personal salvation of individual men..."[61] Flowers says much the same:

> The context of Romans 9 involves individuals and covers the topics of election and salvation, but the context must be examined in order [to] understand the apostle's intention.... Israel was elected to carry the word of God so that anyone might believe and be blessed. Israelites were not guaranteed salvation on the basis of being a descendant of Abraham.[62]

Second, the context of Romans as a literary unit, and of the entire New Testament for that matter, indicates that if God wants to "find fault" he doesn't have to look very far: All have sinned, i.e., all have resisted his will. If God redeems anyone he's really being exceedingly kind. Finally, it may be that God "raised up" Pharaoh for specific reasons not stated in the text. We know that Pharaoh was an insolent, rebellious, unbelieving man. It seems at least plausible that his insolence and rebellion precipitated the hardening of his heart, and not strictly vice-versa.

In any case, all the text tells us (and all we need to know in terms of the plan of God) is that God did in fact raise up Pharaoh for a divinely appointed purpose. In keeping with the theme of sovereignty, Paul proposes a hypothetical ("what if...") beginning in v.21: It is certainly

---

[61] Robert Shank, *Life in the Son: A Study of the Doctrine of Perseverance* (Springfield, MO: Westcott Publishers, 1975), p. 343.

[62] Flowers, p. 107.

conceivable that God, much like a potter working with clay pots, exercises his own sovereign discretion in setting aside certain "vessels of wrath," so that in the end he might make new "vessels of mercy" – "even us whom he called, not of the Jews only, but also of the Gentiles" (v.24). God is a powerful creator and he can build with all sorts of materials. Thus no one's labors are in vain, not Esau's nor even Pharaoh's. Those particular "vessels of destruction" may in fact never be saved, but before they are finally destroyed God will use even them to accomplish his own redemptive rather than destructive purposes. This too is a demonstration of grace. Otherwise as Isaiah says of Israel, "We would have become like Sodom, and we would have been made like Gomorrah" (v.29).

The Unavoidable Responsibility of Human Beings

Still, if the Bible consisted of nothing but Romans 9:1-29, I for one would have few objections to Calvinism. However, in verse 30 Paul reaches a conclusion that cannot be separated from the entire dialogue leading up to it: "What shall we say then?" I.e., what's the point of all this? "That Gentiles, who did not pursue righteousness, have attained to righteousness, even the righteousness of faith." Echoing the conclusion from Chapter Four, Paul maintains in a larger context that salvation is still by faith. And faith still means two things: (1) *A recognition of man's depravity and God's righteousness.* This is a key part of what Paul has been driving home to this point. The Gentiles found righteousness not by seeking righteousness, that is, in themselves, but by believing the message of God. (2) *A response of human volition or will.* In my opinion, this has everything to do with Paul's conclusion, which answers the big question: why? Why are some saved while others are not? Why did Israel seem to have missed the Messiah? "Because they did not seek it by faith" (v.32).

Now Paul shifts the focus from God's prerogative to Israel's prerogative: *They* did not seek it by faith. According to Shank,

> Israel's failure to 'arrive'…is not at all due to some absolute unconditional decree arising arbitrarily from the fact of the sovereignty of

God, without respect to anything in men. The cause of Israel's present frustration is their own unbelief and disobedience. They have only themselves to blame.⁶³

And though they stumbled in their own pride and ignorance, apparently they had ample opportunity: "...And whoever believes on him will not be put to shame" (v.33). Shank explains further: "Their failure (as Paul affirmed, 9:31-10:21) stemmed from the fact that they sought righteousness by their own works, rather than by faith, thus stumbling over Christ, whom they found an offence."⁶⁴

In my view, an understanding of faith in Paul's argument helps make some sense of the apparently disparate spiritual realities of divine election and human decision that somehow converge at the point of salvation. Faith is not reducible to an expression of God's sovereignty; neither is it reducible to an expression of human willpower or works. Faith is an act of the will, yes, but an act that repudiates the ability of the will to obtain righteousness and instead recognizes the power of God alone to save. In other words, faith is the human acknowledgement of divine sovereignty.

So what is the good news of the gospel? It is certainly not that Jesus died to save *some* of us. The Calvinistic doctrine of limited atonement would be very *bad* news for most of us. No, the good news is that God so loved the world, Jew and Gentile alike, that he gave his only begotten Son, that whoever believes in him would be saved. One would have to distort the clear meaning of John 3:16 to derive a Calvinist reading of the gospel such as, "For God so loved the elect, that He gave His only Son, that whomsoever He had chosen to not perish but have eternal life should believe in Him."⁶⁵

Whatever exactly election may mean, it does not mean *denying* men an opportunity for salvation! Rather, it seems to mean something to the effect that God alone has the moral authority to initiate salvation; and we

---

⁶³ Shank, p. 341.

⁶⁴ Shank, p. 342.

⁶⁵ See Steve Ray, "The Gospel According to Reformer John Calvin," February 2001, <http://www.catholicconvert.com/blog/2011/02/06/the-gospel-according-to-reformer-john-calvin/>.

cannot so much as choose it, much less live it, apart from his grace; and he has decreed from the foundation of the world that those who would respond to him in faith would be saved – and he alone knows who they are. It is a waste of time for us to try and figure out who will finally wind up being saved. Thus the proper response to the gospel is not to speculate on the eternal fate of individuals, but to confess Jesus as Lord and believe that God has raised him from the dead (10:9). Thus sounds the glorious message of chapter 10, that salvation is available to all who will hear and believe the gospel: "For whoever calls on the name of the Lord shall be saved" (v.13).

Moreover, almost as if to ensure that his people do not misunderstand the message and settle into a comfortable Calvinist-Stoic indifference to fate, God has specifically appointed the church with the responsibility of sending preachers into the world to minister the gospel, the hearing of which is essential to salvation: "...And how shall they believe in him of whom they have not heard? And how shall they hear without a preacher? And how shall they preach unless they are sent?" (v.14-15). We are sent to preach that the message may be heard, because "faith comes by hearing" (v.17). On the other hand, the Jews have heard and yet have rejected the same message. Because faith is not automatic, it may be said truly that unbelief also comes by hearing. To put it another way, hearing the gospel is a necessary but not sufficient condition for salvation. The decision to believe for salvation cannot be made without the hearing of the gospel, but equally it cannot be made without the consent of the hearer.

The Inscrutable Plan of God for Humanity

What does this mean for Israel then? "Has God cast away his people?" (11:1) Chapter 11 is a comprehensive answer to that question. One would almost expect Paul to respond with a hearty "yes" here, as would many Christians. After all, Paul has gone to great lengths in preceding chapters to prove that all men are sinners, that salvation is by grace through faith, and that saving faith must have Jesus Christ as its object. In sending Christ to the cross, God has provided the final sacrifice for sins. There is nothing more to be done than to believe in him. The Jews as a people have failed to appreciate any of this. It only stands to reason that God would shrug his shoulders and say, "Hey, I tried. If they don't want to get saved it's their problem!" Paul's response to this is that God's grace is again beyond human understanding, sufficient even for the salvation of persistently unbelieving, "disobedient and contrary people," those who reject Christ. "Even...at this present time there is a remnant according to the election of grace" (v.5). (This should also serve as yet another scriptural warning against judging others. Who are we to say who's going to heaven and who's not?) So the pattern of grace repeats itself. Just as God had a remedy for the fall of man in Christ, he now has a remedy for the Jews' rejection of Christ. It is again fully dependent on God's election and grace, and this time God's instrument to open the eyes of his people is... the Gentiles! "But through their [the Jews'] fall, to provoke them to jealousy, salvation has come to the Gentiles" (v.11).

In an ironic role reversal orchestrated at God's discretion, the Gentiles now enjoy center stage as his elect, so that the Jews, now looking on from the outside, might again call upon the Lord for salvation. The picture that emerges is not of a fixed predestination scheme, but of a highly fluid interaction of aggregate human wills under the wise governance of a sovereign God. With his illustration of Israel as the olive tree and the Gentiles as branches grafted onto it, Paul explicitly cautions against reading human fatalism into divine election:

> You will say then, "Branches were broken off that I might be grafted in." Well said. Because of unbelief they were broken off, and you stand by faith. Do not be haughty, but fear. For if God did not spare the natural branches, He may not spare you either. Therefore consider the goodness and severity of God: on those who fell, severity; but toward you, goodness, if you continue in His goodness. Otherwise you also will be cut off. And they also, if they do not continue in unbelief, for God is able to graft them in again (11:19-22).

The language there suggests open possibilities ("He may not spare you either") depending on human decisions ("if you continue in His goodness"). Therefore the story of God's presiding over salvation history is not over. In the divine plan of redemption, God will again choose Israel in a final master stroke of grace – to bring in a final harvest of Gentiles and then redeem both Jews and Gentiles forever: "For if their being cast away is the reconciling of the world, what will their acceptance be but life from the dead?" (v.15) The glorious resurrection of the entire church is actually contingent on none other than the conversion of the Jews. This perspective of Israel's role in the redemption of the nations serves as an antidote for the arrogance of the Gentiles, who might otherwise be tempted to think of themselves as God's permanent chosen "replacements" for the Jews. As is turns out, God is now using us (Gentiles) to save Israel, in the same way that he used Israel to save us. There are simply no grounds for Gentiles, a "wild olive tree," to boast against the cultivated tree to which they have been grafted strictly by grace. After all, the Gentiles have been brought in "so all Israel will be saved" (v.26).

Paul's astounding conclusion of the entire matter is that God is able to use even disobedience – whether that of Jews or Gentiles – to fulfill his sovereign plan. "For God has committed them all to disobedience, that he might have mercy on all" (v.32). In his great love and mercy, God has determined to save his people. Not even rebellion can stop him! To follow Paul's argument from beginning to conclusion is to follow him right into his spontaneous worship of God expressed in v.33: "Oh, the depth of the riches both of the wisdom and knowledge of God! How unsearchable are His judgments and His ways past finding out!" Paul's argument is much more than a "theological treatise."

Like Stephen Hawking's description of the physical universe, Romans attests to the mind-boggling wisdom and majesty of God. Hawking asks, "Even if there is only one possible unified theory, it is just a set of rules and equations. What is it that breathes fire into the equations and makes a universe for them to describe?"[66] For believers the answer should be obvious. In the same way, the soteriology of Romans is not merely a set of abstract doctrines and principles. It points the way to the living God, who breathes fire into our theology by actively working in the course of history, down to the details of our very individual lives, saving for himself a people called by his name. As Paul continues into the opening verse of Chapter Twelve, such a God is worthy of unreserved praise, worship and obedience: "I beseech you therefore brethren, by the mercies of God, that you present your bodies a living sacrifice, holy, acceptable to God, which is your reasonable service...."

---

[66] Hawking, p. 190.

5. Eschatology: The Present and Future Kingdom

Luke's Gospel records the disciples making a wise and humble request of Jesus: "Lord, teach us to pray." Jesus' wide-ranging reply suggests not only the importance of prayer for his disciples generally, but provides a clue as to the priority of his kingdom in connection with spiritual or supernatural activity. Jesus begins with three essential points of contact in prayer: "When you pray, say: Father, hallowed be Your name. Your kingdom come. Your will be done..." (Luke 11:2). Like Matthew, Luke records the coming of the kingdom as the first specific request to be made by the disciples to the Father in prayer. As with so many of Jesus' sayings, this reference to the kingdom is not incidental but intentional and theologically significant.

To make sense of this sort of "kingdom prayer," we must therefore first understand the central place of the kingdom of God in the New Testament. Jesus preached the kingdom continually and taught about it with numerous parables. "The mysterious breakthrough of the kingdom," says Derek Morphew, "was particularly manifest in the ministry of Jesus, as he announced it, taught it, and demonstrated it, in the cross, resurrection and ascension, and the outpouring of Pentecost."[67]

The Kingdom at Hand

Jesus began his ministry in the first chapter of Mark, for instance, with a kingdom announcement: "The time is fulfilled, and the kingdom of heaven is at hand. Repent and believe the gospel" (Mark. 1:14). The nature of that kingdom is then revealed in the breakthrough of God's power into the usual and mundane routine of everyday life. The multitudes are astonished at Jesus because he "taught them as one having authority, and not as the scribes" (v. 22. The Greek word for "authority" here is *exousia*, which implies power, force, ability, strength, right and jurisdiction.). Jesus casts

---

[67] Derek Morphew, "What is the Kingdom: Implications of the Kingdom," *Vineyard USA Library*, <https://vineyardusa.org/library/what-is-the-kingdom-implications-of-the-kingdom/>. I am much indebted to Dr. Morphew's teachings on the kingdom for the material in this chapter.

out a demon on the heels of ministering the Word, so that the crowds ask: "What new doctrine is this? For with authority He commands even the evil spirits, and they obey Him" (v. 27). Right away we can see a connection between the spoken words of Christ and the miracles that follow.

Luke similarly describes Jesus' inaugural announcement in terms of miraculous intervention and dominion (Luke 4:16-21). Jesus' ministry here can be seen again as the twofold act of declaration and demonstration: (1) "To proclaim liberty to the captives" and (2) "to set at liberty those who are oppressed" (v. 18). Actual deliverance again occurs in the context of proclaiming it. Reading Luke further, we can see the same pattern in Jesus' commission to the twelve, entailing a transfer of spiritual authority from himself to his disciples: "He sent them to preach the kingdom and to heal the sick" (9:2). The disciples obeyed on both counts: "So they departed and went through the towns, preaching the gospel and healing everywhere" (v. 6). In Luke 10:1-9 Jesus gives the same commission, this time to the seventy. So the commission expands a little further, beyond the immediate circle of the twelve. Following Christ's crucifixion and resurrection, Luke again restates the commission, in terms that evangelicals such as you and I have quite rightly taken as applicable to the entire church throughout all ages (Luke 24:45-59; c.f. Matt. 28:16-20; John 20:19-23).

Notice the progression: (1) Jesus announces the arrival of the kingdom in his own person and substantiates it with visible signs and wonders. (2) He commissions the twelve to do likewise: preach the kingdom and demonstrate its power. (3) He then expands this kingdom commission to include the seventy, then the entire church. At no point does the empowered character of the commission itself change; rather, it merely applies to an ever-expanding circle of believers.

The announcement, or proclamation, of the arrival of the kingdom is an act of faith. It follows and works in conjunction with another act of faith, the prayer of the kingdom: "Your kingdom come." Kingdom prayer is an expression of faith and of the manifest will of God. It could be argued that "Your kingdom come" and "Your will be done" amount to precisely the same sentiment. God's will in that case is not a complete mystery (though we know it is never *entirely* within the grasp of our understanding); God's will is that his kingdom would be made manifest in the earth, that the transcendent purposes and authority of God would be established and demonstrated "on earth as in heaven." The early believers prayed the will of God when they prayed: "Stretch out your hand to heal and perform miraculous signs and wonders through the name of Your holy Servant Jesus" (Acts 4:30). Throughout the Scriptures, private prayer determines to some degree the nature of public experience (Ex. 2:23-25; Jer. 33:1-3; Matt. 6:6).

Therefore the prayer of the kingdom expresses the *expectation* of the kingdom. This is why I believe an understanding of kingdom theology (not to be confused with "kingdom *now* theology," or dominionism) is so important. If the church is to fulfill the commission of Christ, we as believers must understand the centrality of the kingdom of God in biblical revelation, and then fully *expect* to see all that Jesus promised in connection with that revelation. On the heels of declaring a theological fact, "the kingdom of heaven is at hand," Jesus issued a command to go with it: "Repent and believe the gospel" (Mark 1:15). God is sovereign, yet acts in keeping with our faith. "According to your faith let it be to you" (Matt. 9:29). Consequently our personal relationship with God, expressed by an active, living faith, is not simply the means to our own salvation but is essential for the expansion of God's kingdom in the earth.

Eschatology and the Kingdom

Students of theology will recognize the last things, or end times, as the proper domain of *eschatology*. Eschatology is a broad area of Christian theology, encompassing such grand themes as the resurrection of the dead and the afterlife, the Rapture, the Great Tribulation, the Second Coming of Christ, the Millennium and the Last Judgment. Erickson has summarized the broad outlines of a biblical eschatology as follows:

All human beings (except those alive when the Lord returns) must undergo physical death, at which time they go to an intermediate state appropriate to their spiritual condition. Those who have trusted themselves to the saving work of Jesus Christ will go to a place of bliss and reward; those who have not, will go a one of punishment and torment. At some future time Christ will return bodily and personally. Then all the dead will be resurrected and consigned to their ultimate destination – heaven or hell. There they will remain in an unalterable condition.[68]

Unsurprisingly, even while there is agreement on these main features of eschatology, there is often considerable disagreement, controversy and strife over the details. According to many New Testament scholars, the kingdom of God is a key, if not *the* key, to understanding eschatology (or at least understanding which parts are most important to understand!). "The Christian revision of Jewish apocalyptic eschatology," says Braaten, "was determined by the modifications which Jesus of Nazareth himself effected through his preaching of the kingdom of God.... The central motif of Jesus' message was the coming of the kingdom of God."[69] More, so the kingdom is the unifying thread of New Testament theology generally. "The kingdom of God…is the true context of most New Testament doctrines. Because Jesus had his focus primarily on the kingdom, and because the kingdom is firstly about eschatology… New Testament doctrine has to take eschatology as its starting point."[70]

The eschatological implications of this kingdom theology are, as they were in the first century, profound and revolutionary. Contrary to certain dispensational teachings, Jesus officially ushered in the "last days" when he declared the fullness of the kingdom present in his own person. As Mark Saucy observes, "Jesus was thoroughly eschatological, but in his person that eschatological kingdom of God is on earth. Jesus is now gathering the community of the last days about him…"[71] Matthew describes the passing of the prophetic mantle from John, a self-described lesser

---

[68] Millard J. Erickson, *Contemporary Options in Eschatology: A Study of the Millennium* (Grand Rapids, MI: Baker Book House, 1977), p. 12.

[69] Carl E. Braaten, "The Kingdom of God and Life Everlasting," in Hodgson & King, eds., p. 332.

[70] Derek Morphew, *Breakthrough: Discovering the Kingdom*, rev. ed. (Cape Town: Vineyard International Publishing, 2006), p. 120.

[71] Mark Saucy, *The Kingdom of God in the Teaching of Jesus* (Dallas: Word, 1997), p. 19-20.

prophet, to Jesus, himself the greatest of all prophets and the greatest fulfillment of prophecy (Matt. 11:11-15).

The scene is indicative of a uniform gospel witness to the final (eschatological) manifestation of the kingdom in Christ. Jesus affirms John as a prophet unsurpassed even among the "major prophets" of the Old Testament, and then draws a significant contrast: "...but he who is least in the kingdom of heaven is greater than he" (Matt. 11:11). He goes on, "And from the days of John the Baptist until now the kingdom of heaven suffers violence, and the violent take it by force" (v. 12). Clearly the kingdom of God had not been fully accessible to the masses until John's ministry, which was that of preparing the way for Christ, the way of entrance into the kingdom. In Luke 16:6 we see essentially the same revelation: "The law and the prophets were until John. Since that time the kingdom of God has been preached...."

In addition to the Gospels, the New Testament epistles reveal a similar understanding of the kingdom made manifest in the coming of Christ. Hebrews, for instance, refers to Jesus as a living sign of the end times: "God...has in these last days spoken to us by His son" (1:1-2). The outpouring of the Spirit on the day of Pentecost in Acts further confirms this view, as Peter interprets the events of that day as a direct fulfillment of the thoroughly eschatological "last days" prophecy of Joel: "...this is what was spoken by the prophet Joel..." (Acts 2:16-21). This would seem to imply that miracles, outpourings of the Spirit, and other evidences of God's power seen in the New Testament should be taking place in the church today – because today is part of the last days. Is it possible, then, that our general failure to see miracles in the church today is simply due to our own general disbelief in miracles? Philosophical presuppositions tend to become self-fulfilling. On one occasion, the disciples asked Jesus why they couldn't cast out a demon. His answer had more to do with their state of mind than with their statements on theology: "Because of your unbelief" (Matt. 17:20).

Kingdom theology suggests that the history of the Christian church (spanning the centuries from the incarnation of Christ to the present) is actually the history of the last days. Naturally, this also calls into question the standard Reformed-cessationist view of church history. I would argue on the basis of both testaments (we'll examine the Old Testament shortly) that there is but one *dispensation* for the church, consistently yet progressively supernatural in character. As we have seen, Jesus heralded the age to come (the last days) at the very inception of his ministry.

Eschatology, then, can be seen as the gradual revelation of the kingdom of heaven in successive breakthroughs: the foreshadowing of the kingdom in Old Testament history, the prophetic foretelling of the kingdom by the prophets, the actualization of the kingdom in Jesus Christ, and the fulfillment of all things in the kingdom to come. To put it another way: kingdom theology means that the entire record of Scripture is eschatological; that all of history is literally, constantly progressing toward final consummation in the plan of God. Church history offers extra-biblical support for this view, in the seeming acceleration of kingdom interventions, or revivals. Whereas centuries passed between the Reformation and the Awakening, mere decades passed between the Pentecostal Revival and the Jesus People Movement, for example, and even fewer years between the recent Charismatic Renewal and the "Third Wave" or "New Paradigm" renewal, arguably still underway, which began around 1994.[72]

The Paradoxical Kingdom

Like so many truths of Scripture, the revelation of the kingdom is at once logical and paradoxical. To see the progression of the kingdom through the ages reveals yet another remarkable testimony to the unity and coherence of the Bible, but at the same time reveals the kingdom itself to be an enigma. Unfortunately, too many theologians seem willing to arbitrarily sacrifice the integrity of the Scripture in order to try and make sense of one or another of the mysteries it contains. Presumably Jesus called such truths "mysteries" for a reason. The very quality of God's mysteries is such that it suits the equally "mysterious" purposes of God's plan of salvation. In the case of the kingdom, part of the mystery concerns the

---

[72] Some have argued that the church is currently in a *fourth* wave. See, e.g., James Goll, "The Fourth Wave of the Holy Spirit Has Begun," April 22, 2016, *Charisma News*, <https://www.charismanews.com/opinion/56670-the-ourth-great-wave-of-the-holy-spirit-has-begun>.

placement of various strands of kingdom teaching given by Christ into some sort of eschatological time frame.

As Morphew has outlined, Jesus and the apostles presented the kingdom as a unified yet manifold unveiling of God's rule, one that can be summarized in four general statements:[73]

(1) *The kingdom will come.* In Matt. 24 and other places Jesus promised that he would come again in his final transaction with this world. At some point in the future, Jesus will at last gather together his elect and subject the wicked and unbelieving to an irreversible eternal judgment. Paul taught much the same in his epistles, particularly 1 and 2 Thessalonians. "For the Lord Himself will descend from heaven with a shout, with the voice of an archangel, and with the trumpet of God. And the dead in Christ will rise first" (1 Thess. 4:16).

(2) *The kingdom has come.* This is the most commonly overlooked tenet of kingdom theology: that the kingdom, with all its power and dominion, has already arrived. Thus Jesus interprets his own miracles as kingdom manifestations: "But if I cast out demons by the Spirit of God, surely the kingdom of God has come upon you" (Matt. 12:28). In response to the Pharisees' inquiry as to when the kingdom would come, Jesus answered that the kingdom is already "among you," or "in your midst" (Luke 17:20-21).

(3) *The kingdom is coming immediately.* Jesus and the apostles stressed the importance of readiness, because the coming of the kingdom is always imminent. In statements that confound many evangelical scholars, Jesus promised his disciples that the kingdom would come in their own generation: "Assuredly, I say to you, there are some standing here who will not taste death until they see the kingdom of God..." (Luke 9:1; c.f. Matt. 10:23).

(4) *The kingdom will be delayed.* In Matthew 25, Jesus indicated that the kingdom would not appear immediately. The parable of the virgins teaches wisdom and patience while the bridegroom delays (v. 1-13). The parable of the talents concerns the settling of accounts of a master with his servants after a long time away (v. 14-30).

All this is in keeping with the "Already-Not Yet" paradigm that became a scholarly consensus position sometime during the early sixties: "The Kingdom of God that Jesus preached came to be seen by many as

---

[73] See Morphew, *Breakthrough*, p. 13.

both realized in the present *and* awaited in the future."[74] Recognizing that the kingdom is indeed a mystery – a concept not easily lending itself to precise definitions and theological compartments – is the key to what otherwise appears a confusing if not contradictory New Testament eschatology. In turn, the key to understanding the mystery of the kingdom is understanding that Jesus is not only King but literally the "living end" (the *eschatos*). He declared this of himself plainly in Rev. 2:8: "These things says the First and the Last, who was dead, and came to life..."

That is, Jesus is the full and final revelation of God and of God's kingdom authority. Further, Jesus' claim to be the literal end-all is a distinct proof of his divinity. To be the final ultimate authority, the beginning and end of all things, is to be no less than God himself. So Morphew states boldly, "The divinity of Christ is most profoundly based on eschatology.... If he is the eschatos, then he has to be God himself, the final judge."[75] The division of the ages in successive yet overlapping kingdom interventions has its unifying thread in the presence and reign of Christ himself.

Viewed in this light, the Incarnation of Christ is the manifestation of the kingdom of God on earth. Just as the Incarnation is a fulfillment of the ancient promise of Messiah, so is a kingdom breakthrough rooted firmly in Old Testament revelation. It's important to realize that Jesus did not spontaneously fabricate his teaching on the kingdom in a theological vacuum. Rather, he developed (*embodied*, really) a preexistent concept, as there are explicit references to the kingdom throughout the Old Testament, beginning with the first mention in the Torah. Exodus features a running kingdom theme, which really begins in Chapter Three when Moses asks God directly, "What is your name?" In response, God discloses the divine name, now rendered in Hebrew script YHWH. Scholars are at a loss as to how exactly the *Tetragrammaton,* as the name is called, was pronounced, but more important is what it means: "I am who I am."

According to Hebrew scholars, the name itself can be read as an assertion of eternal, transcendent being, and implies God's authority to break

---

[74] Saucy, p. 18.

[75] Morphew, *Breakthrough*, p. 79-80.

through into the usual course of human events at any time.[76] Chapters 6-12 of Exodus describe this authority vividly, in Moses' confrontation with Pharaoh accompanied by powerful signs and wonders wrought by the hand of God. Finally, on the heels of a divinely orchestrated victory of the infant nation of Israel over the Egyptian army described in chapters 12-14, Moses and the Israelites break into song. They celebrate the might and majesty of the Lord, the crushing of their oppressors and their own liberation as God's people. By prophetic inspiration, this event is interpreted as a sign of God's sovereign, kingly authority: "The Lord will reign forever and ever" (Ex. 15:18).

The kingdom theme builds further in the Sinai covenant, as God speaks to the children of Israel: "And you shall be to Me a kingdom of priests and a holy nation" (Ex. 19:6). God's covenant with Israel resembles the suzerainty treaties of the surrounding nations, in which a conquering king entered into a compact with the conquered people. Unlike the kings dictating the terms of other suzerainty arrangements, however, the King of Israel – God himself – lived among his people in an unprecedented, highly personal, covenant form of suzerainty treaty. In the conquest under Joshua, God's kingdom expands further via military occupation of the Promised Land of Canaan. Then come the glorious years of kingdom dominion and blessing under the rule of David and Solomon. Like the Exodus, the establishment of the Davidic monarchy follows a specific pattern: a kingdom promise (given to David); the securing of dominion through conflict (spiritual and military); and finally, the golden age of blessing, increase and expansion during the years of Solomon as described in 1 Kings 4:25-28. In anticipation of New Testament revelation, the Davidic monarchy prefigures the thorough impact of the kingdom in every area of life: physical, material, spiritual, intellectual and emotional.

---

[76] I have maintained that the history behind the divine name witnesses powerfully to God's activity in history: "This makes Israel unique, in being the only nation on earth whose present existence cannot be adequately explained apart from some powerful historical interactions with the Almighty. That being the case, the reality of YHWH, the God of Israel, best explains the origins of Israel." – Don McIntosh, "From the Exodus to Pentecost," *Cadre Comments* [blog], March 29, 2017, <http://christiancadre.blogspot.com/2017/03/from-exodus-to-pentecost.html>.

Finally, the kingdom is not only foreshadowed by Old Testament history but is directly tied to the New Testament by the prophets, particularly Isaiah and Daniel. Their declarations of the coming kingdom under Messiah serve to connect Old and New Testament revelation as a single prominent and prophetic theme of Scripture. Isaiah announces the kingdom by weaving together a number of diagnostic kingdom messages: the coming king, the coming Spirit, and the coming salvation to be enjoyed by the new people of God (Isa. 9:6-7; 35; 45:1-5; etc.). Isaiah prophesies the inauguration of the Messiah, an event indicative of kingdom authority in Christ (Isa. 61:1-3; Luke 4:16-21). Moreover, Isaiah spoke of the various manifestations of the kingdom later revealed in terms of the "mystery" of New Testament eschatology. Jesus clearly understood his own ministry in the prophetic context of Isaiah.

Jesus equally clearly saw himself as the fulfillment of the Messianic "Son of Man," Daniel's prophetic revelation of the pre-existent yet incarnate, divine yet human, individual yet corporate personality sent by God to ultimately destroy the sinful kingdoms of the world and establish the kingdom of God. Chapters 2 and 7 of Daniel present a comprehensive view of the history of earthly kingdoms, to be supplanted and superseded finally by a spiritual kingdom. This kingdom was to be ushered in coincident with the advent of the Son of Man himself. Jesus repeatedly identified himself with this Son of Man. As elsewhere in Scripture, Daniel's revelation of the kingdom is a picture of radical breakthrough, dominion and blessing. It is furthermore a reality to be fully enjoyed by believers in Jesus Christ as its rightful possessors.

Throughout both testaments the truth is revealed that a legitimate experience of the presence of God, manifestation of the power and majesty of the kingdom, is now available to all who would believe God for it. Embracing the whole revelation of the kingdom may help us resolve disputes concerning *consistent* vs. *realized* eschatology (the "not yet" vs. "already" views of the end), and heal outright divisions over the timing of events like the Rapture and the Millennium. The important thing is that the kingdom is ours to possess, however and whenever it may arrive. Our job is simply to believe it, proclaim it and receive it by faith. "But the saints of the Most High shall receive the kingdom, and possess the kingdom forever, even forever and ever" (Dan. 7:18).

Receiving, believing and proclaiming the gospel of the kingdom is the mandate of Christ for the church. Have there been excesses and abuses in the name of "kingdom theology"? Of course there have, just as there have been offenses and divisions in the name of "Reformed theology" and "doctrinal purity." Perhaps misunderstanding has arisen over a tendency in the church to view theology in terms of a false dichotomy between the truth of Scripture and experiences of divine power. If the preceding understanding of kingdom theology is true, we are now called to take part in an ever-increasing measure of revival, coincident with the advancement of God's kingdom in time toward his own ultimate purpose in eternity.

II. Instantiations of Christian Theology

6. Building on the Foundations: A Study of 1 Cor. 3:1-15

"There is nothing so practical," the great social psychologist Kurt Lewin once observed, "as a good theory." Lewin argued that in fact there is really no such thing as purely empirical science. Or as he put it, "Science without theory is blind":

> Even from a practical point of view the mere gathering of facts has very limited value. It cannot give an answer to the question that is most important for practical purposes – namely, what must one do to obtain a desired effect in given concrete cases?.... This means that theory and facts must be closely related to each other.[77]

A similar principle applies in theology. The *indicatives*, or propositional truths, of theology are closely related to the *imperatives* of how those truths shape human lives and behaviors. In a sense theology is theorizing about God: who God is, how God acts, what God has to say to us and what God expects of us. These questions concern our "big picture" of reality, or worldview. Given the almost self-evident premise that how one thinks about the world impacts how one behaves in the world, theology is eminently practical.

First Corinthians is one of the more practical books of the New Testament, so it offers clear if sometimes disheartening examples of this "applied theology." Following customary greetings, First Corinthians opens with Paul, never one to shy away from conflict, directly confronting the problem of divisions in the church. From there the apostle tackles various issues one by one and in the process shows the impact of theology on life. Paul first counters the Corinthians' petty bickering, personality cults and faction-forming in the first two chapters by exalting the cross of Christ above the wisdom of men.

Chapter Three, which includes the subject passage for this study, builds on these themes with a comparison of men with God as pertains to spiritual and congregational growth, and a portrayal of Christ as the only

---

[77] Kurt Lewin, *Principles of Topological Psychology* (New York: McGraw-Hill, 1936), p. 4.

foundation for spiritual life and eternal hope. Chapter Four continues further with the same basic thought, redefining apostles as weak and foolish servants of Christ rather than strong leaders or spiritual superstars. Paul then addresses in succession through chapters 5-16 the issues of sexual immorality, pagan lawsuits, marriage, conscience, leadership, sin and idolatry, general order in the church, spiritual gifts, love, prophecy, bodily resurrection, and financial support for the saints in the churches.

As a discrete unit of text, 1 Cor. 3:1-15 lends support to two major themes of First Corinthians. First is Paul's continual placing of the apostles in perspective, not as a superior or elite group of leaders, but as servants, fellow workers, small parts of a large body, fools for Christ's sake, and even the "scum of the world." This thought is central to 1 Corinthians, addressed pointedly in chapters 1-4, 9, 11 and 12. Paul expresses the thought in our passage: "What then is Apollos? And what is Paul? Servants through whom you believed..." (3:6). Second is the matter of eternal perspective, the understanding that what really counts is what will never perish. The basic thought is expressed in 3:15: "If any man's work is burned up, he will suffer loss; but he himself will be saved, yet so as through fire." Paul touches on the idea again in chapter 13, in promoting love above all other virtues and gifts as an eternally abiding reality (13:8-13). He elaborates on this issue in both practical and philosophical terms in chapter 15. "Now this I say, brethren, that flesh and blood cannot inherit the kingdom of God; nor does the perishable inherit the imperishable..." (15:50).

Again 1 Corinthians 3:1-15 is a distinct pericope marked by certain textual boundaries. Chapter Three opens with the transitional phrase of verse one, "And I, brethren, could not speak to you as to spiritual men..." The "and" here is a primary article, indicating in conjunction with the remainder of verse one ("I...could not speak to you as to spiritual men..."), a change of subject in sharp, ironic contrast with the preceding discussion of the hidden wisdom of Christ granted to the apostles. Paul assesses the Corinthians' central problem as one of spiritual immaturity, which he identifies through the evidence of one of its main manifestations, personality worship.

He then demonstrates the superiority of the work of God to that of the apostles, via the metaphors of planting and building, both of which elevate God himself as the driving center of any eternally meaningful spiritual enterprise (vv. 5-11). This leads into the thought of building for eternity, and Paul's concluding statement on the matter: "If any man's work is burned up, he will suffer loss; but he himself will be saved, yet so as through fire" (v. 15). Verses 16-17 introduce a closely related but separate topic, of the believer(s) as the temple of God, another "work" subject to being destroyed if not built on the foundation of Christ alone (v. 11). These verses seem to warn of the possibility of eternal loss of the very souls of those "believers" who by their self-destructive behavior demonstrate that they may not in fact believe in Christ. In any case, this small section introduces a separate thought from the previous discussion of building on the right foundation, applicable to sincere but immature believers.

Difficult and significant portions of this portion of this text begin with the meanings of the main metaphors: those pertaining to milk and sold food, planting and watering, the master builder, God's field, God's building, the foundation, and the basic construction materials of gold, silver, wood, hay, etc. Questions which may arise include how, if "no man can lay a foundation other than the one which is laid, which is Jesus Christ," the church can be referred to elsewhere as "having been built on the foundation of the apostles and prophets..." (Eph. 2:20). And what does it mean to be saved "so as through fire"? On the face of it, this verse seems to somehow imply degrees of forgiveness or salvation. That leads in turn to the question of what exactly is meant by "work." If it means the same as does "works" in Romans 3, for instance, then Paul's words here could possibly be read as a promotion of legalism.

History, Culture and Genre

It's clear from even a cursory reading of First Corinthians, particularly its overall color and tone, that Paul is disappointed and distressed over the immaturity of the church in Corinth. History provides a few clues as to why this should be so. The book of Acts records that when Paul arrived in Corinth from Athens (ca. AD 50), he met with a couple, Aquila and Priscilla, who had recently moved to Corinth because the emperor Claudius had driven all the Jews from Rome (Acts 18:2). This bit of earliest Christian history was preserved by the Roman historian Suetonius in his *Life of Claudius*: "He expelled the Jews from Rome, on account of the riots in which they were constantly indulging, at the instigation of Chrestus." F. F. Bruce adds, "''Chrestus,' a common slave-name, was a popular mis-spelling of the name of Christ."[78]

As background information for the founding of the church in Corinth, this incidental reference by Suetonius helps further establish a couple of key facts of early church history: (1) By AD 49, Christianity had already become a highly influential movement throughout the Roman empire. (2) As described in the New Testament, the Jews were openly and physically hostile to the Christians. Indeed, the Jews of Corinth brought Paul himself before Gallio, the Roman proconsul, in order to accuse him - and then beat him after hearing Gallio's disappointing verdict (Acts 18:12-17). Nonetheless, Paul worked diligently to found the church in Corinth, working as a tentmaker, teaching, and preaching for a year and a half in the face of repeated conflicts with the Jews and even his own fears (Acts 18:1-17).

Against this setting, Paul's frustration with the carnal-minded Corinthians is perhaps more understandable. For Paul and many other Christians, genuine faith in Christ was literally a matter of life and death, requiring courage, humility, faith, love, self-sacrifice and separation from the world. Yet despite Paul's best efforts to provide them with the "solid food" of spiritual instruction (v. 2) and a model of Christian behavior, the Corinthians were blending in perfectly with their pagan environment, proudly boasting of their own worldly wisdom, dividing themselves into factions, suing one another in the Roman courts, engaging in the worst forms of sexual immorality, partaking of the communion meal as if it were an all-you-can-eat (and drink!) buffet, and exalting the apostles above the risen Christ. Their behavior and Paul's indignant response calls to mind Israel's sensuous idol-worship in the desert, and Moses' denunciation of their sin. In fact, Paul in Chapter Ten warns the Corinthians of falling into the very sins of Israel in the wilderness (10:1-13).

Paul's insistence that Christ is the only foundation for a life of faith constituted a radical alternative to the philosophy and lifestyle of a Corinthian culture abounding in idols, pleasures and amusements. Just outside the financially prosperous trade city stood the temple to Aphrodite, the

---

[78] F. F. Bruce, *Jesus and Christian Origins Outside the New Testament* (Grand Rapids, MI: Eerdman's, 1974), p. 21.

goddess of love, reportedly surrounded by any number of temple prostitutes. This cultural background might help explain some peculiarities of the Corinthian church. It could be argued that the Corinthians' penchant for idolatry translated directly into their elevation of particular church leaders such as Paul, as well as their easy acceptance of sexual immorality.

First century cultural and economic factors would also explain Paul's selection of the agricultural and architectural metaphors as familiar rhetorical devices for depicting God's building of the church on the foundation of Christ. Greeks and Romans were especially proud of their architectural achievements. And Paul's reference to fire as an eternal means of testing work was especially suited to a first century Greco-Roman audience attuned to the philosophy of Greek naturalists such as Heraclitus, who believed that of the four basic elements (earth, air, fire and water), fire was primary and universal, the chief element of creation, war, change and judgment. There is good reason to believe the Corinthians were well-versed in Greek culture and philosophy generally, since Paul counters Epicureanism in chapter 15 (as he did in Acts 17), quoting the dramatist Menander in the process: "Bad company corrupts good morals" (v. 33).

One of these evident philosophical influences upon the Corinthians was almost certainly a sort of incipient Gnosticism. Whereas Gnosticism became a full-blown heresy in the second century, it seems to have found an early foothold in Corinth. This is the conclusion I came to in my review of Derek Morphew's teaching on Gnosticism:

> Not only did a large faction of the Corinthian church promote the notion of superior wisdom.... Paul laments further that they had endorsed "spiritual" truth to the extent that they were indifferent to bodily sins like fornication, and even denied the reality or importance of the physical resurrection of Christ. Read in this light, First Corinthians becomes a powerful apostolic commentary on Gnosticism...[79]

On the other hand, this position should not be overstated: "While a number of interpreters agree that the teaching that Paul rejects has elements of

---

[79] McIntosh, *Transcending Proof*, p. 106-107.

Gnosticism, most reject the idea that a roving band of Gnostics has invaded the house churches of Corinth."[80]

First Corinthians may also be read as part of the larger genre on the Pauline epistles. This is important, for understanding where the literary unit in question fits into its genre aids further in the process of interpretation. We may assume, as an understanding of this genre (and the text itself, in this case) warrants, that Paul was familiar with this particular audience and was addressing issues particular to their situation at the time of the writing. So depending on the historical context, the instruction given in the letters is often as specific and practical as it is universal and theological. For instance, in First Corinthians Paul consistently downplays his own importance as an apostle, deferring to the undisputed centrality of Christ in response to the particular problem of personality cults and divisions in the church at that time. But later, as recorded in Second Corinthians, influential parties in the church revolted against Paul's authority altogether and he found himself having to defend his ministry and the importance of his own apostolic leadership. Thus certain of Paul's statements about himself which serve to bring understanding in the first epistle would have only served to cause confusion in the second.

Theological Understanding

Paul in 1 Corinthians 3:1-15 offers a number of significant contributions to the larger biblical-theological context, beginning with a theological solution to the problem of divisions described repeatedly in First Corinthians. The Corinthians are divided over a singular issue: Who is the greatest of the apostles? Paul in effect peers into the minds of the believers in Corinth and dares to ask the question of himself and Apollos that others within the church had been asking among themselves all along: "Who is Paul? And who is Apollos?" (These mildly sarcastic rhetorical questions develop the same theme begun in Chapter One: "Has Christ been divided? Paul was not crucified for you, was he? Or were you baptized in the name of Paul?")

---

[80] Jerry L. Sumney, "Studying Paul's Opponents: Advances and Challenges," in Stanley Porter, ed., *Paul and His Opponents* (Boston: Brill, 2005), p. 13.

One can almost see the Corinthians reading this, searching Paul's answers for a subtle defense of his own superiority, or the primacy of his calling, perhaps coupled with a critique of the methods of Apollos. Instead, Paul's answer is that in light of who Jesus Christ is and in light of eternity, the question of who Paul is (or who Apollos or Cephas is) becomes irrelevant. Thus he at once defuses the question, reveals the key to unity, discloses the eternal implications of misplaced faith, and places the entire matter in proper perspective. In so doing, he demonstrates genuine spiritual maturity, which he then recommends for the church in various places throughout the letter.

Within the corpus of Pauline literature, this passage contributes to a balanced understanding of apostolic authority, as a necessity for the church, but something given by God's grace on trust rather than on the basis of outstanding human leadership qualities. Paul sees himself as a "wise master builder" involved in a vital enterprise, yet only "according to the grace of God which was given to me" (v. 10). He defines his very calling in terms of grace again in Eph. 3:8: "To me, who am less than the least of all the saints, this grace was given, that I should preach among the Gentiles the unsearchable riches of Christ." The declaration of v. 11, that "no other foundation can anyone lay than that which is laid, which is Jesus Christ," speaks in context of the danger of building a life on the false foundation of a mere man.

Even Paul's defense of his own leadership in 2 Corinthians is based solely on the authority of God rather than his own greatness, for God's power, he says, "is perfected in weakness" (2 Cor. 12:9). So while Paul never goes so far as to deny the validity of his own apostolic authority – to the contrary, he consistently affirms it – he still links it with human weakness rather than strength, so that God may be glorified rather than men. This helps clarify the meaning of Eph. 2:20, which describes the church as "having been built on the foundation of the apostles and prophets," and makes it clear that the remainder of the verse, "Christ Jesus Himself being the corner stone," is no afterthought but a central tenet of Pauline theology.

Likewise, Paul's metaphors in 1 Cor. 3 contribute to a number of theological themes within the New Testament. His reference to "meat" or "solid food" as a picture of spiritual instruction finds a parallel in Jesus' words to Satan in the wilderness: "Man shall not live by bread alone, but by every word that proceeds from the mouth of God" (Matt. 4:4). The word of God is solid spiritual food, as is his will, so that maturity has to do with obedience to the express will of God. Jesus, like Paul, ties together the concepts of eternally enduring spiritual food with the work and the will of God: "My food [*meat*, NKJV] is to do the will of Him who sent Me and to accomplish His work" (John 4:34). The writer of Hebrews expresses precisely the same thought concerning milk and solid food as does Paul: "For though by this time you ought to be teachers, you have need again for someone to teach you the elementary principles of the oracles of God, and you have come to need milk and not solid food" (Heb. 5:12).

Along related lines, the fact that Paul and Apollos are merely "servants through whom you believed" is in keeping with the larger New Testament principle of leadership exemplified in servanthood, as taught by Jesus: "...and whoever wishes to be great among you shall be your servant...for even the Son of Man did not come to be served, but to serve, and to give his life a ransom for many" (Mark 10:42-45). Peter defines pastoral leadership in terms of service, exampleship and humility (1 Pet. 5:1-5). It comes as no surprise, then, that Paul sees limited intrinsic value in his and Apollos' respective labors: "I planted, Apollos watered, but God was causing the growth" (v. 6).

Spiritual growth is ultimately an act of divine grace: "God causes the growth.... You are God's field." Jesus taught the same principle in the parable of the growing seed: "The kingdom of heaven is like a man who casts seed upon the soil; and he goes to bed at night and gets up by day, and the seed sprouts and grows - how, he himself does not know" (Mark 4:26-27). Elsewhere Jesus portrays the relationship of his disciples with himself as that of branches to a vine, and concludes, "apart from Me you can do nothing" (John 15:5). Paul indicates that the only worthwhile works of men are those which will pass the test of eternal judgment, and so he captures the essence of Jesus' teaching on eternal priorities: "But store up for yourselves treasures in heaven, where neither moth nor rust destroys, and where thieves do not break in and steal; for where your treasure is, there your heart will be also" (Matt. 6:20-21).

Most importantly, Paul emphasizes the preeminence of Jesus Christ himself as the single, ultimate foundation of our faith and our hope of heaven. This truth is reflected throughout the Bible, from the many messianic glimpses of Christ in the Old Testament to the close of the book of Revelation. "Therefore thus says the Lord God, 'Behold, I am laying in

Zion a stone, tested stone, a costly corner stone for the foundation, firmly placed. He who believes will not be disturbed'" (Isaiah 28:16).

Exploring Paul's teaching in 1 Cor. 3 has proven revelatory for me personally, as it runs counter to some of my own long-standing theological assumptions. For years I was taught (and I firmly believed) that following strong, centralized church leadership was the essence of discipleship – a mark of maturity and the key to unity in the church. Even the text of 1 Cor. 3 was interpreted for me within the presupposed context of a hierarchical church structure and a "discipleship" program to go with it. For instance, Paul's denunciation of factions in the church was sometimes read as a general call to unity. In turn, this unity was thought to have been achieved through submission to Paul's leadership and teachings. Consequently, by a subtle shift of emphasis it was believed that one of the functions of the leader is to enforce unity or agreement with his doctrine by appeals to his own authority. Such teachings may be found in the writings of Hobbes and Machiavelli, or even early church fathers such as Ignatius, but not in the NT. Paul in effect says precisely the opposite, that an undue focus on a man (even himself) is an indication of carnality, and will eventually lead to dissensions and factions in the body of Christ. The highest function of church leadership is not to enforce a false unity based on its own authority, but to encourage a true unity by leading men to the higher authority of Jesus Christ himself.

Contemporary Relevance

As an American myself, I can't help but notice that Paul's audience, the church community in Corinth, exhibited a number of characteristics in common with those of postmodern America. The Corinthians lived in (and were clearly influenced by) a permissive social culture, especially as pertains to sexual behavior, yet they prided themselves on their spirituality. As a result, they tended to separate spirituality from truth. The result was a false spirituality evidenced by gifts, manifestations and "tolerance" rather than by faith or love or obedience. Much of what passes for Christianity in America bears a remarkable similarity to the pseudo-intellectual, pseudo-spiritual religion of the Corinthian church. For example, the Corinthians actually boasted of their permitting of sexual immorality in the church, apparently taking great pride in their broad-minded acceptance of other lifestyles. Paul rebuffed this mindset, exposing it as arrogance rather than humility and a dangerous leaven bound to eventually spread throughout the church: "Your glorying is not good. Do you not know that a little leaven leavens the whole lump?" (5:6)

Like Americans, the Corinthians were part of a self-driven litigious society, preferring action in the courts to forgiveness and general civility (6:1-7). Intellectually, they viewed the resurrection of Christ is "spiritual" terms, suggesting that whether Christ rose bodily from the dead is literally immaterial. By extension, they didn't seem too concerned over the fundamental identity of Jesus Christ. Many so-called believers even in Christian churches assert the same, that what matters is not whether Jesus is really God, or whether he really did miracles or rose from the dead, but the practical usefulness of his ethical teachings. Again, there seems to be little distinction between their philosophy and that of the surrounding secular world. Paul countered that the resurrection of Christ is the historical basis of our faith, so that if Christ did not in fact rise our faith is to no purpose (15:13-17).

On another front, the conservative-Evangelical Christian church world at large is beset by divisions. Some of these divisions have to do with perceived matters of essential doctrine and can scarcely be avoided, but many more reflect the particular Corinthian problem of personality worship. Churches are taken in by what Charles Colson has termed the "pedestal complex," an exaggerated reverence for leadership. Christian pastors and television personalities vie for the title of "God's anointed," while the saints in the pews sit back, clap, laugh, and let them perform. All the while, new denominations and movements are constantly splintering off from others as a direct result of supposedly irreconcilable differences between these spiritual leaders. It seems, then, that First Corinthians would provide an excellent source of life issues for preaching to a contemporary American audience.

The text itself implies that while division in the church is a problem, it is actually symptomatic of a deeper problem of spiritual immaturity, or carnality. I would suggest, therefore, on the grounds of verses 5-9, that genuine Christian growth and solidarity cannot be based on a human personality. I cannot even trust myself. Humans all have one thing in common, according to Paul – they are nothing in themselves, since all they have and all they achieve derives from the grace of God. Unity must be based on a common Christian understanding of what is really most important.

This leads into my final thought, from verses 10-15, that despite the many and substantial differences among Christians, we are actually defined by one common belief: that Jesus is the foundation of our faith. A Christian at bottom is a believer in Jesus Christ. Apostles, pastors and teachers come and go, but Jesus is our ultimate authority. This thought could be extended beyond the question of church authority to matters of circumstance, money, ministry, success, family, and ultimately, eternity. Putting our faith or hope in anyone or anything besides the risen, living Christ is really an act of the flesh. On the other hand, a foundational faith in Jesus Christ is a true expression of the Spirit, and brings a proper perspective to critical issues of salvation, ministry and growth in the kingdom. That perspective is eternal. If everything associated with this world is destined to burn, as Paul assures us, the highest expression of faith would be to begin examining our work and building our lives on the foundation of Jesus Christ for the world to come.

7. And the Word Was God: An Exposition of John 1:1-18

Like the other Gospels, the Gospel of John has endured the test of time. "When we recall," says Ernest Musekiwa, "that a very small percentage of books survive more than a quarter of a century, that a much smaller percentage last for a century, and that only a very small number live a thousand years, we at once realize that the Bible is a unique book."[81] Almost 2,000 years since their publication, the Gospels' accounts of the teachings and miraculous ministry of Jesus still inspire and instruct the church. There are a number of reasons for this remarkable staying power – most obviously and most importantly, because the Gospels are more than a mere sampling of literature, but God's inspired message of hope and salvation to mankind.

Also like the other Gospels, the Gospel of John presents the truth of the gospel of Christ to sinful men in need of a Savior. In addition to its practical, spiritually redemptive merits, however, the Gospel of John in particular shows signs of long reflection and painstaking theological development. This highly developed theology is one of a few reasons most scholars consider John the latest of the Gospels. One almost gets the impression from studying it that the principal author of the fourth Gospel (the Apostle John, in my opinion) – like a research physicist writing a book for a lay audience – is deliberately condescending to a level at which everyone can understand. In other words he's translating a rich, divinely inspired revelation, the fruit of a lasting relationship with Jesus himself, into simplified, logically codified terms. (John 21:25 lends support to this view, as the author assures readers that there is much more to the revelation of Christ than could ever be recorded in the pages of a book.)

Nowhere is this combination of simplicity and profundity in John's theology better demonstrated than in the Prologue, the first eighteen verses of the Gospel. In these few verses John masterfully distills some difficult but important theological concepts (the Deity of Christ especially) into a memorable and coherent form.

---

[81] Musekiwa, p. viii.

108 | Transcending Vision

Overall Structure, Themes, and Concepts

An examination of contexts reveals that John 1:1-18 is a well- defined pericope, written from a seemingly detached perspective and consisting of richly theological commentary on the Incarnation of Christ. (Verse nineteen begins what may be termed more typical Gospel material, the story of Jesus' ministry on earth.) The first of four major sections of the Gospel – a Prologue, the signs, the passion, and an Epilogue – the Prologue is not so much a subsection of Gospel narrative; rather it serves as a grand cosmological-theological backdrop or introduction for the events that follow:

> The awesome nature of the Gospel of John takes its character not least for the way it starts. Matthew begins his gospel with a genealogy tracing the lineage of Jesus back to a human being – Abraham. Mark commences with a quotation from Isaiah and introduces John the Baptist while Luke outlines the divine pronouncement of the coming Messiah and circumstances into which John and Jesus were born in Palestine. John takes a different approach. He uses a cosmogony as the background for his message of salvation.[82]

So John, logically enough, begins with the ultimate beginning of all things and ends with the end of all things. Jesus Christ is the answer on both counts. He is the transcendent, eternally preexistent Word (v. 1-3) as well as the fulfillment of grace and truth in human flesh (v. 14-18). In between he is the Light of the world, the truth received by many and rejected by still more (v. 6-7). In a characteristically straightforward manner, John uses the Prologue to pronounce exactly what his Gospel is all about and where his own theological priorities lie.

To expand it a little further structurally, the Prologue may also be seen as a broad synopsis or summary of the entire Gospel itself. This is a uniquely Johannine feature, as there is really nothing equivalent to it in the Synoptics. An implicit structure derived from the Prologue-as-summary view consists of three basic categories, all centered on the person of Jesus Christ: (1) Verses 1-4 are the revelation of Christ, as creator and Light of

---

[82] Gheorghe Dobrin, "The Introduction of the Concept of Logos in the Prologue of the Fourth Gospel," *Perichoresis*, 3, 2 (2005), p. 109.

the world, roughly corresponding to John 1:19-6:71; (2) Verses 5-11 describe the rejection of Christ as Messiah by the Jews, corresponding to John 7-12; (3) Verses 12-18 convey the reception of Christ by his disciples, those who received him and remained with him by faith, as described in John 13-21. In providing a carefully structured overview of events, the Prologue provides further evidence of a deliberate, reflective process of redaction particular to John among the Gospels.

A number of recurring themes in John's Gospel as a whole also appear in the Prologue. Foremost among these are certain cosmic dualistic[83] concepts similar to those common among the Qumran community as recorded in the Dead Sea Scrolls. Light versus darkness is a theme that figures heavily into both the Gospel of John and 1 John, as a metaphor for truth versus deception, spiritual/moral understanding versus ignorance. The two are essentially incompatible: "and the light shines in the darkness, and the darkness did not comprehend it" (John 1:5). It follows that there are only two kinds of people: those who receive Christ and those who reject him (v. 11-12). This too is an expression of cosmic dualism. John also writes from the standpoint of *realized eschatology*, the idea that much of what is generally regarded in the Synoptic Gospels and elsewhere as reserved for the future is actually present reality.

From John's perspective, judgment, salvation and eternal life are not merely distant possibilities to be realized in the course of a prearranged eschatological schedule but are to a great degree realities accessible in the present. In the first chapter John describes Jesus as the "light of men," who "gives light to every man," who gives "the right to become children of God" to "everyone who believes." This is really absolutist terminology, offering little in the way of further eschatological contingencies in order for all men to be fully redeemed. Jesus is therefore the ultimate fulfillment of prophecies and principles of both testaments: "And of His fullness we have all received, and grace for grace. For the law was given through Moses, but grace and truth came through Jesus Christ" (v. 16-17).

The centrality of Christ in John's thinking is unequivocal, and relates to another prominent theme of the Prologue, the deity of Christ. John 1:1

---

[83] John's depiction of cosmic dualism (light v. darkness) should not be confused with the Gnostic conception of spiritual/material dualism, which entails the belief that physical matter is evil. The author of John was clearly not a Gnostic, in declaring that "the Word [spiritual] was made flesh [physical]."

is arguably the strongest affirmation of the divinity of Jesus in the entire NT – which may explain why this particular text is so often interpreted and translated so badly (by Jehovah's Witnesses and others). In a radical departure from his relative contemporaries Philo, Josephus and the Greek philosophers, John carefully crafts his language to assert that in the beginning, at the point of creation itself, the Word (*logos*) already existed. "In the beginning was the Word." The use of the past imperfect in the original language is no accident, but implies a continual state of preexistence on the part of Christ, so that it would really make no sense in reference to any created being. The Word has always transcended the bounds of time and space, and moreover has been eternally "with God," or in the Greek "face-to-face with God" (*pros ton theon*). The Father and the Word have always been in a continual close relationship. The Trinitarian implications of this are unmistakable.

But John continues in the same verse, as if to forestall any speculations of polytheism, "and the Word was God" (or as it was originally penned, "God was the Word"). Certain critics of Trinitarianism argue that the absence of the definite article preceding *theos*, or God (which if included would read "the God") implies that the Word was "a god," perhaps one of many. That objection fails on two counts: (1) Absence of a definite article does not entail any meaning associated with the use of an indefinite article. In fact, there is no article preceding *theos* whatsoever in the clause in question. (2) If John were to assert that "God = the Word" and "the Word = God," and that is all there is to it, then he would not be an orthodox Trinitarian but a Sabellian, and further would directly contradict his previous statement that the Word was "with" God, i.e., distinct from the Father in some sense.

John seems to have gone out of his way to declare the deity of Christ while at the same time steering clear of a reductionist "oneness" or "Jesus only" heresy. His is a three-pronged declaration of deity: Jesus has always existed; Jesus has always existed with or alongside the Father; and Jesus was (or is) God himself, equal to the Father in that respect. Such an interpretation of John 1:1 is further supported by the context of the Prologue in verse eighteen, in which Jesus is the living revelation, literally the *exegesis*, of the Father: "No one has seen God at any time. The only begotten

Son... He has made Him known." The whole of the Gospel likewise provides contextual support of John's affirmation of the deity of Christ (c.f., John 6:20; 8:58; 14:9; 20:28).

Language, History and Literary Development

A number of key terms used throughout John's Gospel can almost all be found in the Prologue, and thereby bolster the thesis that the Prologue summarizes the whole. As we have seen, the "Word" or logos is the creative element and revelation of God himself incarnate in Christ. *Logos* is for the Greeks the rational principle of reality, for the Hebrews the principal agent of creation (as revealed in Genesis 1), and for the early church the message of salvation – meanings all encapsulated in verse 1 of John and paralleled in Hebrews 1:1-2. The term "know" (whether *ginosko* or *oida* in Greek) is used a total of 118 times in John, and can refer to both subjective and objective knowledge. John indicates in verse ten and eleven of chapter one, as throughout the Gospel, that real knowledge belongs to those who believe and receive Christ rather than to worldly philosophers or even the scribes. "Life" (*zoe*, or spiritual, eternal life) is another important term in John's theology, as it is taken most literally: Christ is life itself, so that those who don't believe in him are dead in a very real sense. "In Him was life, and the life was the light of men" (v. 4).

Similarly, Jesus as *Logos* is the "truth" incarnate (v. 14, c.f. John 14:6). On the heels of his post-resurrection accounts, John also indicates that "belief" is central to the purpose of the Gospel: "...but these are written that you may believe that Jesus is the Christ, the Son of God, and that believing you may have life in His name" (John 20:31). That same thought is expressed in verse twelve of the Prologue: Jesus gave the right to become children of God "to those who believe in His name." Finally, there are frequent appeals in John to the "witness" of third parties to substantiate the claims of the Gospel, in compliance with the Old Testament requirement: "By the mouth of two or three witnesses the matter shall be established" (Deut. 19:15). The Scriptures themselves (or "Moses"), the disciples, the multitude, the Spirit, and the Father all bear witness to the authority of Christ. In the Prologue John invokes the witness of John the Baptist: "This man came for a witness, to bear witness of the Light, that all through Him might believe" (v. 7).

One of the keys of interpretation has to do with ascertaining the particular circumstances in which the author wrote, or the historical-cultural context. Certain polemical elements in John's writings, along with much related historical evidence, indicate that his presentation of Christ has been inspired to some extent by conflict. Much of his Gospel, like the Synoptics in this regard, is taken up with polemics against the powerful leaders of the Jews: the Pharisees, the Sadducees and the Sanhedrin. In their general hostility to the message of Christ, the Jewish leaders represent the secular world as well. (Notice how careful John is to record the direct involvement of both Jews and Romans in the crucifixion of Christ, for instance.) Though the conflict develops more vividly in later chapters, John alludes to it in verse eleven of chapter one: "He came to His own, and His own did not receive Him" – and again in verse seventeen: "For the law was given through Moses, but grace and truth came through Jesus Christ."

Among the Gentiles, Gnosticism was one of the earliest and most formidable heresies to face the early church, taking on two main forms: Docetism and Adoptionism. John goes to some lengths to repudiate both strains of Gnosticism in the Gospel and in his letters, especially 1 John. In the Prologue of John, he describes in no uncertain terms the spiritual, eternal divinity of Christ (v. 1-3), as against the Adoptionists, and then proceeds to declare that the same divinity has been fully embodied in human flesh (v. 14), in repudiation of the Docetists. Textual and historical evidence also points to the existence in the apostle's day of a John the Baptist sect (John 1:21-23; 3:27-30), which maintained itself long after John the Baptist's ministry and death (Acts 19:1-3). Like certain Christians today who preach condemnation, these devout followers of John the Baptist seem to have either doubted or ignored the central message of their master. John the apostle subtly counters their influence by way of reminder: "There was a man sent by God, whose name was John. This man came for a witness, to bear witness of the Light.... He was not that Light, but was sent to bear witness of that Light" (John 1:7-8).

Scholars are divided over the issue of authorship, but most agree that John's Gospel was written in stages: (1) The document was originally drafted in light of the testimony of an original apostolic witness – whether actually written by John the apostle himself or by another John, "the Elder" (as he designates himself in 1 and 2 John). Textual evidence in light of Palestinian archaeology favors the "traditional" theory of Irenaeus, citing

Polycarp, that the Fourth Gospel was written by John the apostle of Christ, the son of Zebedee, at Ephesus. (In any event that theory seems to fit better with the facts than the alternative view attributed to Papias by Eusebius, that the anonymous "Elder" wrote from Asia Minor after the Apostle John was already dead.) (2) The core material of the Gospel was subjected to a process of theological development, or redaction, with clear polemical objectives in mind (John 20:31) – which indicates a retroactive or reflective viewpoint. (3) Some would also argue that John was further polished by an editorial group from Ephesus, as indicated by a reference to the first-person plural in John 21:24: "and we know that his testimony is true." As a whole, the high theological development of the Prologue itself is evidence of sustained reflection. This would further lend support to the view that John underwent a number of developmental phases.

John's Gospel, the Letters of John, and the Synoptics

Related to the authorship issue are the striking similarities in John's Gospel to the letters, particularly 1 John. There seems to be no evidence that 1 and 2 John have been edited by an overseeing board of any sort, so that (in my opinion) the overall language, theology, and other similarities between John's Gospel and letters would appear on those grounds to support a theory of single authorship of both. Specific parallels between John's Prologue and 1 John include, as mentioned, a strong anti-Gnostic element. Internal evidence from 1 John indicates an ongoing and even intensified effort on the part of the author to combat Gnosticism. Not one to beat around the bush, John translates his general assertion of the deity and humanity of Christ ("and the Word became flesh") from the Gospel into a litmus-test of the faith in 1 John: "...Every spirit that confesses that Jesus Christ has come in the flesh is of God, and every spirit that does not confess that Jesus Christ has come in the flesh is not of God" (4:2-3). John's confessional statement – "In the beginning was the Word... and the Word became flesh and dwelt among us, and we beheld His glory" (v. 1, 14) – has a direct parallel to the opening words of 1 John: "That which was from the beginning, which we have heard, which we have seen with our eyes, which we have looked upon, and our hands have handled, concerning the Word of life - the life was manifested..." (v. 1-2). In both texts the Word is divine ("from the beginning") and yet is fully human ("became flesh" or "was manifested"). Dualistic concepts in John surface as well in 1 John.

While the incompatibility of light and darkness, for instance, is a major theme of John's entire Gospel, including the Prologue, so it appears in 1 John (1:5-6; 2:8-11).

Among the Gospels, John's uniqueness has long been recognized by Bible scholars and is really accentuated by the Prologue to John. So how does this text in John relate to the Synoptics? To begin, the Prologue itself has no real parallel in the Synoptics whatsoever. Matthew and Luke each preface their respective Gospels with an abbreviated genealogical record, while Mark basically jumps right into the story with the preaching of John the Baptist in fulfillment of OT prophecy. John, much to the contrary, leads into the story of John the Baptist with this profound theological commentary. John's Prologue also introduces a number of terms and themes which contribute to an almost systematic theological treatment of the Gospel record. For John, one might be tempted to say, history is incidental and theology (or Christology) is central – in other words history properly understood points us to the ultimate theological reality, Christ himself. This is especially true of John's Prologue:

> The Prologue, therefore, commences a presentation of the person of Christ, which is quite different from that of other Gospels. It is theological rather than biographical or historical in its approach. It asserts that Jesus, the historic personage known to man, is the Ultimate Fact of the universe."[84]

More so than the Synoptic writers, John seems to place a higher priority on theology than the purely objective recording of historical events. (In fact, he might be inclined to argue that a purely objective record is impossible to obtain in the first place.) This is one reason Clement of Alexandria referred to John as a "spiritual Gospel" rather than an historical Gospel.

Of course, John was in all likelihood aware of the Synoptic material already in existence, and arguably was under no compulsion to produce what would have become essentially a fourth Synoptic Gospel. For failure to recognize his situation, John is too often misunderstood as a mystic, or even as a Gnostic. As we have seen, no one is more opposed to Gnosticism than John. So he's not one to be easily pigeonholed. On the other hand,

---

[84] Dobrin, p. 109

John's theology is fully orthodox, and this is where his alliance with the Synoptics is indisputable (and his differences with them overstated). Where it counts the most, the Gospels are in complete agreement. Jesus is the center of attention. He is the Son of Man, preceded by John the Baptist, anointed by the Spirit, who teaches with authority and not as the scribes and Pharisees, who feeds the multitudes, who preaches the truth so as to open the eyes of the blind, who is delivered up by the Jews and crucified under the authority of Pontius Pilate, and who rises from the dead in victory. Thus John's Prologue could be seen not only as a summary of his own Gospel, but as a basic statement of the gospel message of all four evangelists and attested by the entirety of Scripture.

8. Theology at the Fringes: Miracles, Dreams and Visions

So far, I have tried to ground my theological positions on objective criteria: accepted facts, long-held doctrinal traditions, responsible interpretations of Scripture, and the insights of accomplished scholars. What I will describe below, to the contrary, are personal recollections of highly unusual, almost completely subjective spiritual experiences I've had over the years. I count these experiences as "theological" only because they collectively, if indirectly, bear witness to certain truths of Scripture. I remember very clearly the events to be described in the brief chapter to follow. My more skeptically-minded readers will have to decide for themselves whether I am telling the truth about those events.

I should mention up front that the accounts to follow would have to be considered false *a priori* according to a certain school of theology known as *cessationism*. As Peter Masters explains, cessationism may best be defined in confessional terms:

> The term *cessationism* comes from the great 17th-century confessions of faith, such as the Westminster and Baptist confessions. These both use the same word. Speaking about how God has revealed his will and committed it to the Scriptures, the confessions say, 'Former ways of God's revealing his will unto his people being now ceased'. This word does not actually come from the Bible, but the doctrine does. [85]

For the cessationist, who denies the possibility of miracles in the present day altogether, it is somehow infinitely more likely that all the accounts of miracles in the church today are false, then that his own interpretation of certain New Testament passages might be misguided. Whether they do so consciously or not, cessationists generally follow the same line of reasoning as the most skeptical of philosophers. David Hume in particular argued

---

[85] Peter Masters, "Cessationism – Proving Charismatic Gifts Have Ceased," *Sword and Trowel*, 2011, 2, <http://www.metropolitantabernacle.org/Christian-Article/Cessationism-Proving-Charismatic-Gifts-have-Ceased-Sword-and-Trowel-Magazine>.

that "no testimony is sufficient to establish a miracle, unless the testimony be of such a kind, that its falsehood would be more miraculous, than the fact, which it endeavors to establish."[86] Clearly I neither agree with Hume's extreme skepticism of miracles nor share his confidence in human understanding of exactly how the laws of nature work.[87] For similar reasons I do not share the cessationists' confidence in the unquestionable veracity of their own interpretations of biblical statements, statements which appear on their face to suggest not only that God has performed miracles but will continue to perform them whenever and wherever he pleases. "He who believes in Me," said Jesus, "the works that I do, he will do also; and greater works than these he will do, because I go to My Father" (John 14:12). On its face this suggests the possibility of miracles continuing to the present, as does Hebrews 13:8: "Jesus Christ is the same yesterday, today and forever."

I should add here that I do not *chase after* miracles and seek signs. To the contrary, the handful of experiences related in this chapter were mostly unexpected, punctuating a Christian life of over thirty years that has otherwise been largely unremarkable and uneventful. I begin, though, with a bizarre experience that actually occurred *before* my conversion.

Highway to Hell

Already a troubled, insecure, heavy drinker at around the age of twenty, I was travelling South down Highway 77 on my way from Houston to visit my family in the Rio Grande Valley during the summer of 1984 (or maybe it was '83). I was tired, running late, and depressed even

---

[86] David Hume, *An Enquiry Concerning Human Understanding* (New York: Barnes & Noble, 2005), p. 89. (Originally published 1748.)

[87] I have argued elsewhere that the textbook depiction of science is contradicted by what Kuhn referred to as "scientific revolutions," in which popular and even empirically successful theories become overthrown with the ongoing accumulation of unwelcome data: "If the [scientific] realists are correct to say that falsification of an empirically successful theory is akin to a miracle, then the history of science itself suggests that belief in something akin to miracles is quite warranted." – McIntosh, *Transcending Proof*, p. 88.

more than usual from drinking too much that day. To make matters worse, traffic had slowed to a crawl around Corpus Christi due to road construction. Glancing at my map, I decided to take a detour that led to a little-used farm road, FM 666. (No, I'm not making that up; FM 666 can still be located on a map today.)

Unfortunately, and possibly owing to too many beers in my belly, I had somehow turned the wrong way onto FM 666 and started heading almost directly North, away from my destination. I had already driven a mile or two down the road when I realized my mistake. In a burst of rage I slammed on my brakes, all alone on this quiet, desolate stretch of farm road. When I came to a stop, with gravel dust and the smell of burnt rubber still hanging in the air, I looked up toward heaven and began screaming obscenities at God. It wasn't just that I was having a bad day. My life was a complete disaster, and as far as I was concerned it was entirely God's fault. I knew that God existed, and I truly hated Him for permitting my life to sink so low.

After I put my car back in gear and turned it around, I saw a large black bird of some kind standing motionless in the road a few hundred feet ahead. That alarmed me. This was back when the "Omen" movies were still relatively fresh in the public memory, and this black bird standing in front of me called to mind a scene from one of the movies in which a raven had attacked a young lady and plucked her eyes out. I crept up close to the bird, probably a vulture, and had to practically push it off the road with my car.

Slowly picking up speed and heading back to the main highway, I felt a great dread begin to creep over me. I suddenly realized the significance of what I had just done. I had just blasphemed God with all my heart. I interpreted the stubborn black bird in my path there on FM 666 as a literal *omen* that I had committed an unforgiveable sin. As far as I knew at the time I was doomed to an eternity in hell. Unsettling as this "encounter" with spiritual darkness was for me, it set the stage for my conversion just a year or two later.

Healings

I can only recall two times in my life that I would be willing to state under oath, "I was healed by God and I don't believe anything else can explain what happened." Following my conversion to Christ in 1985, a miracle in its own right, I was attending a tiny Pentecostal church a few blocks from my apartment. We were having a series of "revival meetings" with an evangelist from out of town. The second night there, I believe, the evangelist said that someone in the assembly was suffering pain from a tooth and he wanted to pray for that person. Now my tooth had been in more or less constant but dull pain for a few days, but it didn't hurt terribly, not enough to visit the dentist or tell anyone about it anyway. So I waited for someone else to step up to the front.

Again the evangelist asked if anyone had a sore tooth. And again I glanced around at the other dozen or so members of my church. Finally I decided he might be talking about me, and went up for prayer. The man smiled, prayed for me, and when he was done, asked how my tooth felt. To my surprise it felt fine. I was surprised not only because I felt no more pain, but more so because I experienced no feeling of power or any deep sense of God's presence. My tooth just stopped hurting – and as it turns out the pain never returned. But I was also surprised at the event itself, because before that time I didn't think God bothered with "little" miracles like healing a mild toothache.

I experienced another and altogether more dramatic miracle of healing in 1987. As the spring semester at UT Austin was drawing to a close I was way behind in my studies. Still a relatively new believer, I had become consumed with all things Christian: the Bible, Christian music, Christian books, prayer, fellowship, evangelism, and lots of church activity. Consequently I had let other important matters slip – like my coursework. I had failed to prepare at all for my upcoming final exams. So a couple of days before the tests I began to cram. I wound up studying with such intensity and for so long that I couldn't manage to sleep, not before the exams and not afterwards. As if stuck in some sort of cognitive infinite loop, my mind kept reviewing the same material from my textbooks despite my best efforts to think about other things. Meanwhile what had been an annoying headache from the previous few days slowly became a pounding migraine, one that resisted all forms of relief and further ensured my failure to sleep.

In great pain and increasing desperation, but without a doctor, health insurance, cash, or any idea whom I could call for help, I knelt over on my bed and faintly whispered a simple prayer: "God please heal me… I know you can do it." A few seconds or maybe minutes passed (I don't really remember), and then I sensed the loving presence of God in the room with me. I heard a kind of "rushing" sound, something like the sound of a seashell when you place it in your ear. Then I saw – whether physically or in my mind's eye I'm not sure – what I would describe as an inverted grayish whirlpool spinning above me. I then "saw" strings of letters and words, numbers and formulas, slowly circle around and finally disappear into the vortex of this strange whirlpool. This image or vision, whatever it was, then vanished. I looked around and I was alone in my bedroom. All was quiet. My headache was gone and my mind again began to process thoughts like normal. I lifted my hands high and began to praise God loudly for his awesome power and great mercy. Following this miracle I dedicated myself to God and his calling upon me in a deeper and more serious way.

Gifts of the Spirit

In the 1992 movie *Leap of Faith*, one of the devices used by the phony "faith healer" Jonas Nightengale (played by Steve Martin) to deceive and then defraud his audience was to speak out "words of knowledge," telling visitors personal details about their lives. To pull off this trick, the ministry team first invited visitors to fill out information cards, purportedly so the church could contact and pray for them. Nightengale was equipped with an earpiece, however, so that his fellow swindlers could whisper the information to him: "Woman in red, sixth row aisle seat. Has back problems." Nightengale would then "call out" the woman and reveal his knowledge of her back pain.

Leap of Faith was a comedy, but unfortunately many of us have experienced similar shenanigans taking place in God's name. It may be, in fact, that the film was based on the real life of televangelist Peter Popoff, who along with his wife was caught performing precisely the same stunt and exposed in 1986.[88] Because of this sort of thing the general public has become wary of the whole idea of gifts of the Spirit. That's really unfortunate, because genuine gifts of the Spirit still operate today. Or at least the fact that charlatans and false prophets often thrive in our midst (just as

---

[88] See Al Seckel, "God's Frequency is 39.17 MHz: The Investigation of Peter Popoff," University of Colorado at Boulder. Originally published in *Science and the Paranormal,* 1987. <http://casa.colorado.edu/~dduncan/pseudoscience/PeterPopoff.htm >.

Jesus and the apostles warned would be the case) does nothing to delegitimize genuine gifts of the Spirit. Paul put it this way: "For what if some did not believe? Will their unbelief make the faithfulness of God without effect? Certainly not! Indeed, let God be true but every man a liar..." (Rom. 3:3, 4).

That said, I can recall a number of very specific "words of knowledge" given to me over the years, a couple of which I will recount below. The first occurred in 1988, in El Paso, Texas, when a pastor named Paul Campo picked me out from an audience of some four hundred people and told me that the way out of the paralyzing fear and deep dejection I was feeling was not to strive or contend for a breakthrough, but to *wait* on the Lord. As I now know, but certainly did not know then, I was in the throes of a major clinical depression, the first of many in my adult life. (At the time I thought I was simply losing my mind, or possibly possessed by a horde of demons.) Anyone familiar with clinical depression knows that apart from medication or a miracle the only "cure" available is time. Struggling against it only makes it worse, and usually prolongs recovery. Holding fast to that word over the next few months helped me hang on until – in what I then considered a *bona fide* miracle – the depression slowly began to subside on its own so many months later.

Another memorable word was given to me, in 1994 I believe, when Tricia and I were struggling to get our little Pentecostal church off the ground in Lubbock, Texas. An evangelist from California named Crea Copeland was preaching for a sister church in Hobbs, New Mexico. We were friends with the pastor in Hobbs, so we went up for the service. At the end of the service Crea called me out and said that there was a certain area of town where I had been thinking about really concentrating my evangelistic efforts. "Cast your nets there," he told me.

When the meeting was over, I went over to him and told him how remarkable that word was, because I had, in fact, been thinking a lot about completely focusing my work in a certain part of town – though it wasn't all that close to our church building. He then said, "Are there are lot of apartments there? Because that's what I saw." That part floored me. The very reason I wanted to start preaching in the area mentioned was that we had not been well received in the various residential neighborhoods around our church building. Though I had not told anyone, not even my wife, the area I was looking at was basically so many blocks of nothing but apartment complexes. True to the direction provided by Crea's ministry, we began doing outreaches in that neighborhood, and sure enough, began to see people repent, surrender to Jesus, and become involved in the church.

Snow Angel

Around 1993, again during our time pastoring in Lubbock, Tricia and I headed out to Amarillo for a winter Bible Rally. The region had been hit with unusually heavy snow, so that parts of the highway between the two cities were packed hard with snow and ice. I had picked up Tricia and our new convert friend, Abel, straight from work, in hopes of getting to the rally more or less on time. Because we were behind schedule, I was unfortunately pushing my little 1985 Nissan pickup a bit harder than I should have. At some point we hit a stretch of solid ice and lost control. Fishtailing back and forth for some way, my truck at last made contact with a patch of brown earth off the side of the road. Immediately the truck flipped over completely on its side, then half-flipped again to land upside down in the snow.

I crawled out my window, and the first thing I saw was Abel climbing up out of the passenger side window. I didn't see Tricia, but I heard her calling my name with a distinct note of distress in her voice. She kept complaining that she couldn't move her leg. I then realized she was trapped under a pinched section of the dashboard. Worse, we were both keenly aware that she was four months pregnant. She began to cry and asked me what we were going to do. I didn't have the slightest idea what we were going to do. All I could think to do was pace back and forth in the cold, muttering "God help me, God help me" in a daze.

At that point a man appeared in front of me. I remember that he had dark hair and was wearing a black Harley-Davidson T-shirt on top of whatever else he was wearing. He walked right up to me in the snow and said, "Don't worry. You believe in God, right?" I said yes. "Well he's going to help you. I've already called 911 and an ambulance is on the way" (this was before everyone carried cell phones). Then he stepped closer to me and said something to this effect: "Now you need to get back over there and be with your wife. She needs you to be strong for her." Still somewhat dazed, I nodded in agreement and turned back to the truck. Then I realized I hadn't thanked him. So I turned around again to say thanks…but no one was there. I did as he had said, though, and told Tricia that help was on the way, that God was going to help us, and that everything was going to be okay. In a few minutes the ambulance arrived as the man had said; and emergency technicians managed to extricate Tricia from the truck using a "Jaws of Life" hydraulic rescue device. She had suffered a fractured pelvis, and had to hobble around with the aid of a walker in the weeks to follow, but gradually recovered and gave birth to a healthy, handsome baby boy five months later.

Before that day I had never given too much thought to angels. I still have no idea how they are supposed to look, or exactly how they might be expected to interact with human beings. But I am convinced that on that day, if at no other time in my life, I had a very brief and very important conversation with an angel.

Dreams and Visions

Generally I don't take much stock in dreams, because most of the dreams I have are completely irrational, fragmented, and difficult to recall. Once in a while, though, I have a dream that is not only strikingly vivid and coherent, but spiritually significant. Quoting the prophet Joel, Peter in the book of Acts declared,

> And it shall come to pass in the last days, says God,
> That I will pour out my Spirit on all flesh;
> Your sons and daughters shall prophesy,
> Your young men shall see visions,
> Your old men shall dream dreams... (Acts 2:17)

With an understanding that some dreams spring from the outpouring of the Spirit, I will go ahead and share some of my dream experiences. One of the more disturbing dreams I ever had, some three or four years ago, could be described as a "tour of the underworld." What I remember of the dream began inside a giant, dark and dirty auditorium-like structure. There I saw countless men, moving about frantically and chaotically, darkened by shadows, continually striving and contending with one another. Most of these men were busy jostling for the best spot in their section of the building or for prominence in their particular little group. If someone showed signs of weakness the others would attack him. Sometimes they would all start physically assaulting each other without the slightest provocation. Most were recognizably human but many were disfigured in some way. One creature had four arms instead of two, and was off by himself, posing and flexing his muscles for no one in particular to see.

Then I saw something like a dungeon. There men on the ground level were stripped naked under a spotlight, their bodies glistening and their heads hung down in deep shame, while other men gathered in a sort of balcony above were gawking at them and catcalling to them. In my dream I knew that these men were sex slaves. I understood that in that place the purpose of sex was not to express love, nor even to experience pleasure. Sex was strictly a means to exercise power and degrade others.

In the next "scene," so to speak, I found myself in a large room, again with men clamoring and scurrying around with no evident purpose. Suddenly a creature with the bearded face of a man but the body of a furry animal, like a fox or a badger, appeared above the room, flying (though without wings). He was the only one there with the power of flight, and everyone stopped and looked up at him. In the dream I was privy to the fact that he believed himself incomparably handsome and glorious. The look on his face was so smug that I remember thinking it was comical. But no one there was laughing. Indeed, all the other creatures feared this one greatly. I gathered that this was Lucifer. Though I saw no flames, I knew then that I was observing hell itself.

Finally I realized that I did not belong and could not survive in this place, so I began searching for an escape. I headed toward a large opening at the perimeter of the building and to my amazement simply walked outside. There were no guards and no one else was outside. (I'm now reminded of something C.S. Lewis once remarked, that hell is actually locked *from the inside*.) I trudged through some muddy, marshy ground under thick clouds for a while, and then broke out into a flatter, firmer sunlit area where I perceived myself to be free. Then I awoke.

A few years back, maybe 2013 or so, I had a dream that Jesus was returning. Here's how it went: I was standing alone by a lake, behind which stood a large hotel or condominium overlooking it. As I looked around enjoying the view, a bolt of lightning unexpectedly flashed across the sky. That caught my attention, so I kept looking up. Then I saw a large flock of black birds begin to fly across the lake and then suddenly fall towards the earth dead. Right after that I saw a message begin to appear in large white letters in an unknown language across the sky. I realized in a moment that Jesus was about to return, not just soon, but *that day*. Without waiting to see more I sprinted to the building behind the lake, where I saw a number of my friends inside (not friends I can identify, but people I knew to be friends in my dream). I tried to warn them of what was happening, but none of them would pay attention to me because they were looking down at their smart phones, texting, reading posts on Facebook or watching videos. I yelled louder but they would either ignore me completely or glance up at me quickly and nod, and then go right back to their phones. I understood this to mean that my friends were so captivated by *this* world that they simply could not see a need to prepare for the next. There the dream ended.

I have also experienced some horrific, overtly demonic nightmares. What's interesting here is that most of these more terrifying dreams can be traced to an idol or graven image somewhere in my house. Let me explain. If a magazine, say, or a travel brochure arrives in the mail showing images of Hindu gods, and I go to sleep, I will have one of these nightmares. In fact, when I do have one of these terrifying dreams, I can almost always do a search of the house and find the object or image causing the trouble (my wife can attest to this).

After the worst nightmare I've ever had – I woke up with my heart beating so furiously I feared dying on the spot – I found a cheap plastic baby doll lying nearby with a defective eye that my daughter had picked up from a bin full of similarly defective dolls at a dollar store. I had to break the doll in two and put it outside before the sense of terror left the house. Almost always, once I toss the offending image in the trash and take it outside, I sleep peacefully. Other times I am haunted by nightmares but cannot find any idols or religious images in the house. In those cases I can usually find an offending image or message posted somewhere on my Facebook page or email account, and simply delete (or unfriend) the source. Again I sleep peaceably afterwards. These instances always serve to remind me not only of the stark, powerful reality of spiritual warfare, but of the jealous love God has for his children.

Finally, I should mention that a few of my dreams have been edifying and encouraging. While working at Home Depot around 2005, on two separate occasions I dreamed that a coworker got promoted, and told the person. In each case the man had been frustrated in his career for many years, and in each case he was promoted within a few months. My wife and I have had similar dreams about my own career advancement, one particular in which we were honored together at some sort of banquet by my employer – though I wasn't sure who the employer was or what prompted the occasion. Maybe one day that dream will come to pass and then we can find out.

Depressions, Dangers and Deliverance

I've often said that in my Christian life I have experienced not only my greatest joys and triumphs, but also the most severe of hardships and perils. I think deliverance and recovery from these situations often qualify as miracles. In 2 Cor. 11, the apostle Paul "boasted" of the many infirmities, afflictions, trials and persecutions he suffered for Christ's sake, and listed some of them out for his readers. I will take the rest of this chapter to do something like that.

My first highly excruciating trial of faith began in 1987, while a college student and a day or so after my spring finals. I had just been quite suddenly and miraculously healed of the worst headache I'd ever experienced and was ecstatic about it. Just a few minutes later, though, my mind was suddenly subjected to a long and powerful barrage of evil, blasphemous thoughts. I couldn't stop these thoughts and had no idea where they were coming from (though I know now!). The resulting confusion, guilt, and anxiety led me down the path of a deep, suicidal depression – the first of many such episodes I was to experience.

As a result of the sleeplessness, inability to concentrate and general dysfunction that characterizes a major depression, I soon found myself dropped out from school, fired from my job at a Bennigan's restaurant, and then evicted from my apartment. With the help of my pastor, Frank – who had no idea what was happening to me but could tell it was deadly serious – I found a tiny, $175-a-month efficiency apartment in a sketchy, well-worn neighborhood in Austin. That was a pretty scary place for a nervous, depressed, bookish type like me. But it was there that I slowly began to recover.

During my three years in that dingy little apartment I witnessed fistfights, an attempted suicide, an attempted mugging, and people smoking dope openly on the walkways around my unit. My neighbor Les had his car stolen, while I was fortunate enough to keep the remainder of my car after my $600 Alpine stereo was lifted from it. I was once knocked to the ground by a drunk Vietnam vet tenant next door who complained that I was acting "superior" to him by going to church. Another time I was attacked by a half-dozen or so teen wannabe gang-bangers who threw rocks at me and jumped me in the apartment parking lot after I shared the gospel with them and cautioned them to repent. They stopped their assault when I screamed for help and Les came out to see what was the matter.

One summer evening I was studying at my desk by the front door when I heard gunshots nearby. After that I heard some shouting in the distance, another couple of shots, and then the shouting getting much closer. I mustered the courage to peek outside my window, and some 20-30 feet away saw a gang of men, one of them stomping on the parking lot pavement of my little apartment building and yelling "Crips!" while the others whooped and hollered. I shuddered, turned off my lamp, quietly bolted my door, dropped to the floor and began to whisper desperate prayers for protection and deliverance. A few moments later I noticed that the noise had stopped, so again I worked up the courage to peek out the window. This time all I saw was a blue and white Austin Police sedan driving past. I thanked God for what I still believe was his gracious intervention to protect me and my neighbors.

Besides Les, one of my only friends there was Ralph. A rather compact, older fellow, Ralph had a terrible drinking problem and was covered with tattoos, but he laughed a lot and he was very down-to-earth. I couldn't help but really like him. One evening while reading on my little sofa wearing nothing but a pair of shorts, I heard the sound of glass breaking. I looked out the window, and saw two guys hunched over Ralph on the ground, one with a broken bottle in his hand. Without hesitating (knowing that if I stopped to think I would be too scared to act), and expecting to get horribly injured or killed, I banged open my door and ran straight at the men, screaming at them, "Get out of here!" To my great astonishment they took off running. Rising from the pavement and very drunk, Ralph looked at me and said, "You saved my life." And I believe that by God's grace I did save him. I should have been cut to ribbons by those men, but again I believe God somehow preserved me.

Over the years I have endured many deep depressions, paralyzing fears and night terrors, physical threats, a house robbery, accidents, totally unexpected job losses, and some stunning personal betrayals. Tricia and I have scraped by during seasons of poverty, and we have been abused and publicly slandered by people we thought were friends. But somehow we've managed to cling to Christ, and to each other, through it all. In this we are reminded of the apostle Paul. Towards the end of his life, in prison and awaiting execution, Paul declared that despite much abandonment and hardship, God had been faithful to preserve him for his own purposes:

> But the Lord stood with me and strengthened me, so that the message might be fully preached fully through me, and that all the Gentiles might hear. Also I was delivered out of the mouth of the lion. And the Lord will deliver me from every evil work and preserve me for his heavenly kingdom. To Him be glory forever and ever. Amen! (2 Tim. 4:17-18)

9. Theology Beyond the Fringes: Heresies in History[89]

To the postmodern mind, an investigation of heretical movements and personalities in the history of the church may seem pointless, if not outright divisive. In a time of technological, commercial and cultural globalization, it may seem only natural for the church to embrace and even endorse those many, often well-meaning believers who seek to unite all parties as one under the umbrella of the kingdom of God. Consequently, relatively few pastors and church leaders nowadays have much time or tolerance for apologists, theologically conservative scholars, or "heresy hunters."

The work of *polemics*, the use of reason to confront and debate opposing claims to the truth, has all but disappeared from the church. As R.C. Sproul has pointed out, the fallacies of the "secular" world, including relativism, generally wind up in the "spiritual" church in one form or another: "The mind-set, or rather, anti-intellectual mind-set, of secular education has infiltrated and all but conquered evangelicalism. Evangelicals are sublimely happy to embrace both poles of contradictory ideas and accept radically inconsistent and mutually exclusive theologies."[90]

We believers have no one to blame for this situation but ourselves. The disconcerting fact is that the contemporary church has – in many quarters – simply lost its hold on the truth. In trying to explain the explosive growth of cults in the twentieth century, McDowell and Stewart suggest, "If the church fails to carefully and seriously provide spiritual warmth and a true exposition of the Word of God, those with spiritual needs will find other avenues of fulfillment."[91] The tragedy of that loss becomes all the

---

[89] This chapter is a revised version of a special project written in 2006 for the Trinity Graduate School of Theology and Apologetics, under the supervision of Dr. Johnson C. Philip.

[90] R.C. Sproul, *Essential Truths of the Christian Faith* (Carol Stream, Ill: Tyndale, 1992), p. xx.

[91] Josh McDowell & Don Stewart, *Handbook of Today's Religions* (Nashville: Thomas Nelson, 1983), p. 19.

more apparent when one realizes the tremendous energy committed to its defense by the church throughout the course of history. Moreover, "heresies" often have arisen as little more than sincere attempts at reforming a visibly compromised and corrupted institutional church. Paul Johnson thus observed of the rise of heresies in the Middle Ages, "once belief in the Church's system of confession, repentance, penance and redemption was undermined – no great problem – the only spiritual warrants were the outward signs of chastity, poverty, asceticism and humility, which the official Church, as a rule, clearly did not possess. These the heretics supplied."[92] A study of heresies in history should therefore serve a manifold purpose: to sharpen the intellect, strengthen convictions, encourage a spirit of accountability within the church, and build spiritual defenses. Moreover, a serious investigation of heresy may – paradoxically – help refine our understanding of orthodoxy. After all, the very concept of "heresy" holds no meaning apart from an implied understanding of orthodox, sound doctrine. "Even these departures," said Louis Berkhof, "are important for the History of Dogma, since they often led to a clearer and sharper formulation of the truth."[93]

No less critical is an appreciation for history itself, into which the glorified *Logos*, Jesus Christ, "emptied himself" (Philippians 2:8) to become our salvation, and through the course of which fiercely loyal ministers of the gospel have perennially defended the faith. From the Gospels' historical accounts of the birth, life, death and resurrection of Christ, to the many and varied accounts of the doctrines and experiences of the church, Christianity is nothing apart from the record of history. Josh McDowell accordingly declares what until recent years had always been obvious: "There is no doubt that much of the evidence for the validity of the Christian faith is rooted in history. Christianity is a historically founded faith." Comparing it with historicism, C.S. Lewis defines history, particularly the history upon which Christianity is based, as "a story with a well-

---

[92] Paul Johnson, *A History of Christianity* (New York: Simon & Schuster, 1976), p. 251.

[93] Louis Berkhof, *The History of Christian Dogma* (Carlisle, PA: Banner of Truth Trust, 2002), p. 24.

defined plot..." The imaginative but thoroughly fact-based reconstruction of past events known as *historiography* is at root a social science, an empirically grounded field of research. Yet, as Charles Hedrick points out in his *Ancient History,* to try and conceal personal prejudices and motivations in the writing of history is rather pointless, as "modern academic historians," along with the rest of us, "need to recognize that when they write, even about people as distant as the Greeks and Romans, they always inevitably also write about themselves."[94]

History by any realistic definition cannot be reduced to a scientifically objective account consisting of so many primary and secondary sources, methods, monuments, letters, official documents, coins and inscriptions. Rather, human understandings of history – in this case, the doctrines of the Christian faith – find their expression as personal, if well informed and methodologically guided, interpretations of such evidence. Like the Scriptures themselves, raw historical data have surprisingly little to say apart from honest, rigorous human interpretation. History, then, circumscribes the point at which empirical evidence and religious imagination intersect, and thereby furnishes an ideal medium for defining and transmitting the faith.

Heresy Defined

According to Chas S. Clifton and others, heresies can mean anything from forward-thinking, innovative attempts at reform to outright rebellion against the authority of Christ and His church. Heresy by a most basic definition is deviation from orthodoxy. Using the Scriptures as the "rule of faith," this author holds to biblical-theological conservatism as the best representation of Christian orthodoxy. On the other hand, an adherence to ecclesiastical or "institutional" orthodoxy does not guarantee a foolproof interpretation of Scripture. So, because he had to temporarily play the "heretic" in order to bring reform to the "orthodox," Luther is included here along with other believers whom Protestantism would recognize as fairly orthodox. The Reformation serves as a powerful historical reminder that Scripture itself, and not any particular school of theology that lays claim to it, is and must remain the rule of faith for the church. We do well

---

[94] Charles Hedrick, *Ancient History: Monuments and Documents* (Malden, MA: Blackwell, 2006), p. x.

to recall that the Roman Catholic Church descended directly from the primitive church of the apostles, and yet fell into gross error. Despite the pronouncements of today's Protestant "orthodox," the Reformed church could undergo the same sort of devolution. Heresies litter the landscape of the past, but also promise to endure well into the future. Warned the Apostle Peter, "But there were false prophets among the people, even as there will be false prophets among you…" (2 Pet. 2:1).

Heresies typically exhibit a number of distinct elements in common. Most notably, heresies are remarkably similar to the orthodoxy which they mimic. Though a diehard Roman Catholic himself, Hilaire Belloc was nonetheless on the right track when he said, "Heresy is the dislocation of some complete and self-supporting scheme by the introduction of a novel denial of some essential part therein."[95] That is, a heresy is not some completely unheard of, revolutionary system of thought, but is rather a subtle deviation from the original system in some vital point of doctrine. At the same time it is important to emphasize the "vital" part. Not every questionable doctrine or aberrational teaching amounts to a denial of the Word of God. Unfortunately, for much of church history, any and all deviations from orthodoxy, no matter how slight or trivial, were judged outright as "heresies."

Moreover, heresies – even after being thoroughly refuted and rejected by the church at large – have a well-documented tendency to reappear under various new labels. As the philosopher Santayana declared famously, "Those who cannot learn from history are doomed to repeat it." Berkhof suggests that errors persist only because believers fail to consider their own history in formulating doctrine, so that "ancient heresies, long since condemned by the Church, are constantly repeated and represented as new discoveries."[96] So Gnosticism, fades away at the turn of the third century, but then resurfaces in various modified forms, such as Catharism around the turn of the first millennium, then as Christian Science near the turn of the second. First century Judaic legalism only slightly altered becomes Pelagianism a few hundred years later, then New England

---

[95] Hilaire Belloc, *The Great Heresies* (San Francisco: Ignatius, 2017), electronic edition, originally published 1938.

[96] Berkhof, p. 5.

Puritanism and the works-based "revivalism" of Charles Finney in the eighteenth century. The Docetism (denial of Christ's physical reality) that plagued the early church reappears as "Jesus myth" theories now so popular among twentieth and twenty-first century theologians. And on it goes.

It turns out that the history of heresies in the church has not been "evolutionary" or "progressive," but rather depressingly cyclical. False doctrines have proven nearly as resilient as the gospel message itself. That lesson needs to be burned into the minds of modern believers. Contemporary Christians are called to fight the same good fight as did Paul and fellow apostles John and Peter.

I. The Birth of the Church to the High Middle Ages

First Century

As Berkhof and other historians have illustrated, the early church had to endure not only secular persecution from the Roman state, which came to regard Christianity as a threat to the political stability of the empire, but religious persecution from Jews defending the older, established tradition. Their respective religious belief systems became the chief ideologies competing with the Christian faith, and eventually worked their way into the church itself. Through the process of infiltration, the harsh reality of persecution introduced the subtle root of heresy. To oversimplify things only a little, most heresies can now be divided into two broad camps – legalism and Gnosticism – each with its heretical origins in the first century. This rough working dichotomy will help to organize and classify heresies, and at the same time demonstrate the historical persistence and resilience of false teachings.

The problem of legalism arguably began precisely when the church began, with the conversions of the Jews from the Jerusalem synagogue. James was the undisputed leader of the Jerusalem church, one who evidently had not completely grasped the concepts of Christian atonement and justification. A reading of church history, including the earliest history on record, the book of Acts, makes it clear that orthodox Jews and Greek (Gentile) Hellenists brought much cultural baggage with them into their new Christian experience. Apostles steeped in Judaism, such as James and Peter, had a tendency to relapse into the rigorous rites and demands of the

Old Covenant, so that the Hellenists often found themselves treated as second-class citizens. At the heart of such legalism is always a denial that the work of Christ is sufficient to secure salvation for humanity.

Historian Paul Johnson observes that the object of Jewish persecution was "to purge the movement of its radical wing, end the Gentile mission, exclude the Greek element...and so complete the reabsorption of Jesus' followers."[97] Here the value of Paul's contributions to the doctrinal development of the early church becomes evident. Only a radically, supernaturally converted Apostle Paul had the combination of boldness and religious credibility needed to confront the legalism that otherwise threatened to abort Christianity in its womb. Paul's letters to the Romans, and to the Galatians especially, demonstrate the depth of the Jewish legalism problem in the first century. His message was slow to be accepted, however, even among the leaders.

Not to be outdone, the Gentiles brought into the church a more cosmopolitan if more loosely-defined belief system, what church historians refer to as "incipient Gnosticism." E. R. Dodds explains: "Rather than postulate...a primitive Gnostic system from which all the rest derives, I should prefer to speak...of a Gnostic *tendency* which shows itself already in the first Christian century, notably in the writings of St. Paul, and in the second century finds its full expression in a series of imaginative mythological structures."[98] A number of diverse elements – from secular Greek philosophy to the spiritualism of the pagan mystery religions – help make up the polymorphous Gnosticism that has haunted the church over the intervening centuries. Nonetheless, Gnosticism can be identified by a recognizable set of central operating assumptions, especially dualism. Popularized by Plato four hundred years before Christ, dualism is the idea that reality consists of two distinct, irreconcilable elements: physical and spiritual. Church historian Bruce Shelley contends that Gnostic dualism

---

[97] Johnson, p. 35.

[98] Dodds, E. R., *Pagan and Christian in an Age of Anxiety: Some Aspects of Religious Experience from Marcus Aurelius to Constantine* (New York: Cambridge University Press, 2000), p. 18.

divided the world into "two cosmic forces, good and evil. In line with much Greek philosophy, they identified evil with matter."[99]

Gnostic dualism led naturally to asceticism and elitism, in that its devotees claimed special levels of knowledge into spiritual matters and looked askance at those who could not understand them. Curiously enough, it also led to *antinomianism*, literally "lawlessness," as acts done in "the flesh" were often believed to have no effect on the "spiritual man." Traces of the Gnostic problem in the first century can be detected within the pages of the New Testament itself, from the Gospel and letters of John to the Pauline epistles to the Corinthians and Colossians. John seems to have been dealing particularly with Docetism, a Gnostic-related heresy denying the physical reality of Jesus altogether. Evidence of Docetic teachings can also be found in the letters of Ignatius, a late first century bishop of Rome, who asked, "And if, as some atheists (I mean unbelievers) say, his suffering was a sham (it's really they who are a sham!), why, then, am I a prisoner?"[100] Though Gnostic leaders became more popular in the second century, at least a few made a name for themselves in the first. These include Simon Magus, described in the book of Acts as one "claiming to be someone great" (Acts 9), and Cerinthus, known for his denial of the deity of Christ and his disputations with the Apostle John.

Second Century

Gnosticism continued to gain ground into the second century, as spokesmen such as Basilides and Valentinus further refined and ritualized their teachings, while carefully fusing them together with Christian doctrines. "Along with apostolic Christianity," says Shelley, "they accepted the idea of salvation, the idea of a supreme deity, and the idea of heavenly beings at work in the universe."[101] At the same time, the Gnostics literally distanced the pure and spiritual Supreme Being from the physical, corrupt

---

[99] Bruce Shelley, *Church History in Plain Language* (4th ed.) (Nashville, Thomas Nelson, 2013), p. 55.

[100] Mark Galli, ed., *The Apostolic Fathers* (Chicago: Moody, 2009), p. 95.

[101] Shelley, p. 54.

creation, by ordering the creation as a hierarchical "series of emanations." Berkhof adds that Gnosticism was only able to flourish due to the general religious syncretism that marked the spiritual environment of the early centuries. It also held a certain appeal to those put off by the moral implications of the gospel, and especially to the large Hellenist element in the church. It offered an alternative soteriology, in which select, enlightened men are saved by knowledge of mysteries, rather than by faith in Christ. In keeping with their hierarchical cosmology, Gnostics classified themselves along three tiers of spirituality: the enlightened *pneumatics*, the middle-class *psychics*, and the spiritually dull *hylics*.

More than anything, Gnosticism attempted a serious, if defective, answer to the problem of evil in the world. "To the majority of Gnostics," says Dodds, "it was unthinkable that such a world should have been created by the Supreme God: it must be the handiwork of some inferior demiurge – either, as Valentinus thought, an ignorant daemon unaware of any better possibility; or, as Marcion thought, the harsh and unintelligent God of the Old Testament."[102] Fortunately, even an allegedly more philosophically sophisticated and theologically defined Gnosticism could not check the passionate advance of genuine Christianity. It would experience the same fate as the Mithraism so popular among the first century Romans. Having faced off with the historical Christian faith, and its defenders – such as Irenaeus, Hippolytus and Tertullian – Gnosticism proper lost the battle and momentarily disappeared. Like most heretical notions, Gnosticism would resurface under various guises repeatedly throughout the history of the church.

Of the prominent Jewish-Christian sects, the Ebionites were arguably the most influential. They emerged as a continuation of the Judaic elements who vigorously opposed the Apostle Paul, as first witnessed in Luke's account of the Jerusalem conference (Acts 15) and mentioned so often by Paul in his letters (those "of the circumcision"). From the Gnostics, the Ebionites borrowed the repudiation of Christ's essential divinity in order to, as Berkhof suggests, "maintain Old Testament monotheism." According to the Ebionites, Christ's only real contribution to the salvation of men was a higher interpretation of the Old Testament law. In *Against*

---

[102] Dodds, p. 16.

Heresies, the early bishop Irenaeus complained that the Ebionites "use only the Gospel according to Matthew; they reject the apostle Paul, calling him an apostate from the law..."[103] Eventually, says Clifton, *Ebionitism* came to be used to describe Jewish Christianity with existing links to practicing Judaism, and at the same time "to signify anyone who denied Jesus's divinity and considered him to be only an outstanding moral teacher."[104]

Coming at the problem of Christ's identity from another angle, the Elkesaites (or Elchesaites) affirmed the spiritual superiority, but not the divinity, of Jesus. "Their movement was probably an attempt to gain recognition for Jewish Christianity by adopting it to the syncretistic tendencies of the age," said Berkhof.[105] It could be said that while Ebionitism extended the Jewish legalistic tradition within the church, the Elkesaites offered a more general, cosmopolitan Christianity compatible with just about any belief system on the market. They represented the "liberal," humanistic, pluralistic Jewish elements still thriving in the church today. Hippolytus complained, "They do not... confess that there is but one Christ, but that there is one that is superior *to the rest*, and that He is transfused into many bodies frequently, and was now in Jesus."[106] It should be added that this new, highly spiritual version of Jewish Christianity had much in common with the Gnostic movements afoot at the time.

Third Century

The distinct, spiritually destructive movements and personality cults normally associated with *heresies* began to really develop in the second century and to proliferate into the third. Marcion, a Gnostic teacher who

---

[103] Irenaeus. *Against Heresies*. From Philip Schaff, *The Apostolic Fathers with Justin Martyr and Irenaeus*, Grand Rapids: Eerdman's, 2001, p. 352.

[104] Chas S. Clifton, *Encyclopedia of Heresies and Heretics* (New York: Barnes & Noble, 1992), p. 39.

[105] Berkhof, p. 45.

[106] Hippolytus, *Refutation of All Heresies,* from Alexander Roberts & James Donaldson, *Ante-Nicene Fathers*, Vol. 5 (Grand Rapids, Eerdman's), p. 148.

devised his own canon of Scripture – excluding the entire Old Testament and much of the New – was excommunicated by the church in Rome in AD 144, but his teachings lived on well into the next century and beyond. As Marcion saw it, the God of pure love, pure grace and unbridled freedom could not be reconciled with the "vengeful" deity described in the Old Testament. The apologists, Irenaeus foremost among them, challenged Marcion's presumed superior spirituality and self-appointed authority to single-handedly define the canon. Irenaeus, in writing *Against Heresies,* bitterly opposed Marcion for advancing "the most daring blasphemy against Him who is proclaimed as God by the law and the prophets, declaring Him to be the author of evils, to take delight in war, to be infirm of purpose, and even to be contrary to Himself."[107] In elevating a fabricated "God of love" above the true God of Scripture, Marcion prefigured the antinomianism, moral compromise and theological emptiness that continues to plague the church.

Much the same could be said of the late second century "prophet," Montanus, who along with his sidekicks Prisca and Maximilla went about prophesying and claiming to have fresh revelation equal to that of Scripture. Appearing first among the small, poor villages of Asia Minor during a second century wave of persecution from Rome, Montanism embodied the "super spiritual" excesses first exposed by Paul in 1 Corinthians, and still enjoying a following among many Pentecostals and charismatics. In his *Ecclesiastical History,* the fourth century bishop Eusebius offers a glimpse of stern opposition to Montanism by the church: "And these people blasphemed the whole Catholic Church under heaven, under the influence of their presumptuous spirit, because the Church granted to the spirit of false prophecy neither honour nor admission."[108] On the other hand, it could be argued that the legalistic asceticism and charismatic exuberance of the Montanists actually served as needed reform elements for a church often inclined to laxity, worldliness and self-indulgence. Indeed, such was the influence of the Montanists that the great orthodox apologist

---

[107] Irenaeus, *Against Heresies*, p. 352.

[108] Eusebius, from Henry Bettenson & Chris Maunder, *Documents of the Christian Church* (New York: Oxford, 2011), p. 82.

(and noted anti-Montanist!) Tertullian eventually joined them, to the dismay of the church.

Possibly even more influential, however, were the teachings of Mani, yet another dualist and advocate of a sophisticated new brand of Gnosticism. Philip Schaff refers to Manichaeism as "the latest, the best organized, the most consistent, tenacious and dangerous form of Gnosticism, with which Christianity had to wage a long conflict."[109] Mani's upbringing in the Persian mystery religions, along with Chaldean astrology and Asian Buddhism, clearly bore heavily on his late third century doctrinal distortions of Christianity. Thus Manichaeism features elements not only of a Docetic Gnosticism, but of Buddhist asceticism and pantheism. Mani appears also to have been one of the first anti-Christian cult leaders, proclaiming himself to be, in Schaff's words, "the last and highest prophet of God." Along with many historians, Paul Johnson describes the essence of Manichaeism as pessimistic dualism: "Like Gnosticism, it was dualist. But it was characterized by an intense pessimism about the potentialities of human nature and its inherent goodness, relieved only by confidence in the existence of a godly elite."[110] So widespread was Mani's influence that among orthodox believers *Manichaeism* became virtually synonymous with any dualist heresy. A former adherent of Manichaeism himself, St. Augustine became its most vocal and effective opponent. As Schaff notes, "His nine years' personal experience of the vanity of Manichaeism made him thoroughly earnest and sympathetic in his efforts to disentangle other men from its snares, and also equipped him with the knowledge requisite for this task."[111]

During all this internal division and spiritual strife, the church also experienced waves of external, physical persecution from the Roman state.

---

[109] Philip Schaff, *History of the Christian Church, Volume II: Ante-Nicene Christianity, A.D. 100-325*, Section 135: Mani and the Manichaeans, <https://www.ccel.org/ccel/schaff/hcc2.v.xiii.xxiv.html>.

[110] Johnson, p. 114.

[111] Philip Schaff, *Nicene and Post-Nicene Fathers, Series I, Volume 4: Augustine: The Writings Against the Manichaeans and Against the Donatists*, p. 36. <https://www.ccel.org/ccel/schaff/npnf104.iv.iii.html>.

Like Nero in the first century, the Emperor Decius had singled out Christians as the source of all the empire's troubles, and had instituted a ferocious campaign to extinguish their fire of faith. Many leaders in the church understandably felt the need to distinguish between the real "saints," believers who had suffered for their faith, and those backsliders who had lapsed under the stress of circumstance.

Working initially from the premise suggested by Bishop Cyprian, that "there is no salvation outside the church," spiritual leaders pressured the churches to forbid reentry to those who had denied Christ, on the grounds that they had committed "the unpardonable sin." Though Cyprian himself had decided upon a policy of readmission to lapsed believers, upon exhibiting a spirit of repentance and works of penance, a presbyter named Novatus (or Novatian) insisted that the church could not forgive such gross sins as apostasy. The early church historian Socrates recounted, "Novatus, a presbyter of the Roman church, separated from it, because Cornelius the bishop received into communion believers who had sacrificed during the persecution that the emperor Decius had raised against the Church."[112] In response the Roman hierarchy predictably defended its right to do anything, including forgive sins of the most notorious offenders. The heretical upshot of Novatianism was twofold: believers either held to the legalistic requirements of Novatus, or sought forgiveness from the Catholic Church via the legalistic new sacrament of penance. Another lasting side effect of the Decian persecution was the veneration for the martyrs as saints.

As the church endured challenges both internal and external into the third century, its foremost thinkers began to wrestle with issues of definition, or theological questions. The Alexandrian church fathers, Clement and Origen, had inadvertently contributed to the rise of theological controversies by embracing Greek philosophy, allegorizing Scripture and treating the nature of God and the dual natures of Christ as exercises in mysticism. In opening theological questions about the godhead, and establishing the Alexandrian-allegorical school of interpretation upon Plato and

---

[112] Schaff, Philip. *Socrates and Sozemenus Ecclesiastical Histories* New York: The Christian Literature Publishing Co., 1896.

Philo as much as Jesus, it could be argued that Clement and Origen effectively laid the groundwork for, and thus led the church into, its great theological and Christological controversies.

One of the first noteworthy theological deviations was the *Monarchian* movement. "While the great heresy of the second century was Gnosticism, the outstanding heresy of the third century was Monarchianism," says Berkhof.[113] Like many doctrinal errors, Monarchianism began with the best of intentions, a desire on the part of third century theologians to defend both the unity of God and the deity of Christ. *Dynamic Monarchianism*, popularized by Theodotus of Byzantium, made the godhead a simple, fundamental unity, and therefore reinforced the error of the Ebionites.

According to another Monarchian, Paul of Samosota, Jesus the man was so completely given to the will of the Father that he became gradually "deified," thoroughly imbued with the nature of God. In general terms, Paul of Samosota's doctrine typified the heresy of *adoptionism* – the idea that God conferred deity upon the mortal Jesus. The heresy of Sabellianism, on the other hand, emphasized the integrity of the godhead at the expense of its various "modes" or "manifestations," of which Christ was but one. Sabellius maintained the divinity of Christ, but only by arguing that the Son was actually as much Father and Spirit as they were the Son, all of them equal manifestation of the one God. Tertullian, along with Hippolytus, the disciple of Irenaeus, denounced Monarchianism's various expressions in no uncertain terms. Epiphanius, bishop of Salamis, rejected the "foolishness" of Sabellianism, namely, that "three names are attached to one substance." These doctrines and the disputes which surrounded them led naturally to the Trinitarian controversies of the heresy-rich fourth century.

Fourth Century

The fourth century may be considered one of the high-water marks of heresy. While the Monarchian debates continued unresolved, a handful of new and significant deviant movements rose up around some starkly influential personalities. Arius, especially, deserves special mention among the heretics of history due to the sheer intensity of the debates he fomented.

---

[113] Berkhof, p. 77.

Berkhof observes that because the influence of Arius was so pervasive, "The great trinitarian strife is usually called the Arian controversy, because it was occasioned by the anti-trinitarian views of Arius, a presbyter of Alexandria..."[114] In essence, Arianism applied the Monarchian notions of monotheism and adoptionism to New Testament theology, arguing that because the Son of God was "begotten," he was a created being. In a letter to his friend Eusebius, Arius himself acknowledged that he and his followers were persecuted "because we say that the Son has a beginning, but God is without beginning." According to a letter from the bishops at the Synod of Nicea, Arius was additionally condemned for suggesting that the free will of Christ implied His potential for sin and evil.

So effective was Arius' rhetoric, and so widespread were his views, that they largely precipitated the Council of Nicea in 325, whose delegates, Athanasius foremost among them, issued the famous Nicene formulation as a result: "We believe in one God, the Father Almighty, Maker of things visible and invisible. And in one Lord Jesus Christ, begotten not made, being of one substance with the Father..." It could be argued that Arius served as the predecessor to those many cults which to this day make professions to Christian faith but deny the essential deity of Jesus Christ – from the Latter-Day Saints (Mormons) to the Watchtower Bible and Tract Society (Jehovah's Witnesses).

Just as Novatianism had risen up around the problem of lapsed congregants seeking readmission to the churches following the persecution of Decius, Donatism emerged as a response to the compromises of bishops during the Diocletian persecution. On the face of it, the controversy concerned the validity of bishops who had surrendered up the Scriptures to be burned under pressure from Diocletian's henchmen. At the root of Donatism, however, lay the old problem of legalism. Donatus and his followers held that bishops – even repentant bishops – who had relinquished the Word of God to pagans on demand (for them to burn) were insufficiently holy to minister further in the church. Saint Augustine fought the Donatists stringently, maintaining as always that any "holiness" to which the church, including bishops, could ever lay claim derived strictly from the grace of God. "When baptism is administered in the words of the gospel, however great be the perverseness of either minister or recipient, the sacrament is

---

[114] Berkhof, p. 84.

holy on his account whose sacrament it is."[115] Or to paraphrase Christ's words to the Pharisees, "The Son of Man is lord of the sacraments."

Although the Donatists duly earned the designation of "heretics" by invalidating the reality of grace, history again indicates some fault for the contention on the part of the orthodox leaders, whose luxuriant and even lascivious lifestyles continually provoked sincere if extreme reform efforts by fellow churchmen. In larger terms, Donatism thus represents the sorts of ecclesiastical "stumbling blocks" that traditionally have encouraged heresies and divided the church. As Sean Martin observed, "The moral life of the clergy became the rallying point for reformers, dissenters and disaffected churchgoers alike, and such was their stress on the moral stature of the clergy that the reformers [such as the Cathars] resembled the Donatists…"[116]

It could be said that the Christological controversies, essentially a subset of the lingering Trinitarian issues, began with the teaching of Apollinarius. A pastor from Laodicea, the evidently well-meaning Apollinarius suggested that, as Bruce Shelley describes, "the divine Word (Logos)… displaced the animating and rational soul in a human body, creating a 'unity of nature' between the Word and his body."[117] The result of Apollinarius' sincere effort to refute Arianism, adds Johnson, was "a heresy of his own which denied that Christ had a human mind."[118] Thus Gregory of Nazianzus, Archbishop of Constantinople, warns his hearers not to be deceived by Apollinarians who claim that Christ "is without a human mind." This teaching seems to have emerged not only as a response to Arius, but as a Christology, an attempt to rationalize the Incarnation. In debunking Apollinarius' teaching, leaders such as Gregory revealed also its adoptionist flavor: "If any assert that the manhood was fashioned and afterward endued with the Deity, he…is to be condemned…" With its emphasis on

---

[115] Cited in Bettenson & Maunder, p. 83.

[116] Sean Martin, *The Cathars: The Most Successful Heresy of the Middle Ages* (New York: Thunder's Mouth Press, 2005) [electronic edition].

[117] Shelley, p. 120.

[118] Johnson, p. 90.

rationality at the expense of revelation, Apollinarianism served as a precursor to the overly codified theology of the Scholastics.

Fifth Century

If Donatus had caused Augustine considerable consternation, Pelagius tied him in knots in the early fifth century. The battle between Augustine and Pelagius over sin and grace mirrored the Arian-Athanasian controversy from the previous century in its passion and intensity, and in its lasting effects on the history of doctrines. Probably because of Augustine and somewhat unfairly, Pelagius has been presented as the very embodiment of pride, self-righteousness and legalism in the church. As Johnson says, "Augustine saw in Pelagius a form of arrogance, a rebellion against an inscrutable Deity by an undue stress on man's powers."[119] The errors of Pelagius lay in this "undue stress," that is, in their emphasis more than in any inherent falsity.

Along with so many other heresies, Pelagius' teaching was more reformative and reactionary than rebellious. He seemed less concerned with openly advocating legalism than with pointing out possible abuses of grace under the Augustinian vision – "by imagining," as he says, "that a man will be condemned by [God] for what he could not help; so that (the blasphemy of it!) God is thought of as seeking our punishment rather than our salvation." Despite the fact that he has been accused and condemned for promoting raw legalism and repudiating grace, Pelagius himself confessed, "That a man has this possibility of willing and effecting any good work is due to God alone..."[120]

For Pelagius, the Garden of Eden was therefore more than just a blessed paradise, but a place of precarious freedom – to love and believe God, or to rebel against him and sin. Grace, then, was given after the fall to help man along on his somewhat self-determined journey back to righteousness. These "semi-truths" eventually led many in the church to moral

---

[119] Johnson, p. 119.

[120] Cited in Henry Bettenson & Chris Maunder, *Documents of the Christian Church,* 4th ed. (New York: Oxford, 2011), p. 56.

reform, and to embrace a middle view between Augustine's and Pelagius' now known as "Semi-Pelagianism." Sadly, those same semi-truths left Jesus with no real purpose for sacrificing His life on the cross, and left the questions of sin and salvation unresolved. Augustine accordingly countered Pelagius with the powerfully rhetorical question: "How can a will be free if it is under the domination of unrighteousness?"

As the fifth century progressed, the Christological controversies initiated by Apollinarius began to escalate as well. Apparently in reaction to both the Christology of Apollinarius and the emerging Catholic doctrine that Mary was the "God-bearer" (or "Mother of God"), Nestorius, bishop of Constantinople, countered that Christ received his two natures from his two separate lineages: his divinity came from God the Father, and his humanity from Mary. Consequently, Jesus was basically a vessel housing two separate, almost irreconcilably competing natures. According to Bettenson and Maunder, Nestorius received his teachings from Theodore of Mopsuestia, who illustrated the "conjunction" of human and divine in Christ as something like the union of husband and wife. That is, the "one union" consisted of two distinct personalities with distinct natures.

Paul Johnson remarks that like most heresies, Nestorianism was a reactionary belief, formulated in a time when orthodoxy was most elusive: "A right-thinking theologian, anxious to remain orthodox, tended to smash his ship on Charybdis while trying to avoid Scylla.... Nestorius...reacting from Apollinarianism, reasserted the manhood of Christ to the extent of questioning the divinity of the infant Jesus..."[121] As a result Nestorius was condemned by a synod at Alexandria, upon the urging of its bishop, Cyril. The conflict between Nestorius and Cyril was actually part of a larger conflict between the "Antiochene" and Alexandrian schools of theology, the former tending to emphasize Christ's humanity, the latter his divinity. The fate of Nestorius should also serve as a reminder that false teachings can arise from the best of intentions. False teachers are real men and in some cases, at least at first, even honest and good men.

Discovering the finer points of theological truth turned out to be no easy task. Another "reactionary" fifth century theologian from Constantinople, Eutyches maintained against Nestorius that Christ's nature was wholly unified, almost as if chemically fused together following an initial

---

[121] Johnson, p. 90.

process of union. This too proved unacceptable. Shelley thus summarizes the historical theological situation in terms of so many hair-splittings: "So against Arius the church affirmed that Jesus was truly God, and against Apollinarius that he was truly man. Against Eutyches it confessed that Jesus' deity and humanity were not changed into something else, and against Nestorius that Jesus was not divided but one person."[122]

Along with many heretics, Eutyches' main contribution to the church was incidental and unintentional – in his case, the precipitation of the Council of Chalcedon (451 AD) and its construction of a relatively lasting, definitive Christology. In the "Tome of Leo," the bishop of Rome used his considerable authority (and rhetorical skill) to sway the Chalcedonian council: "Each nature…performs its proper functions in communion with the other; the Word performs what pertains to the Word, the flesh what pertains to the flesh. The one is resplendent with miracles, the other submits to insults."[123] Though the bishops agreed with Leo and ratified their decision with their famous creed, Chalcedon did not entirely succeed. While unifying most elements of what would now be called Catholicism, Protestantism, and even Eastern Orthodoxy, the council repelled certain Christians (Monophysites) who maintained with Eutyches that the human and divine aspects of Christ were mysteriously combined into a single nature. Modern-day descendants of fifth century Monophysitism include the Egyptian Coptic Church and the Jacobite church of South India.

Sixth Century

First emerging in sixth-century Armenia, according to Sean Martin, the Paulicians exhibited a curious blend of Marcionite-Manichean dualism-adoptionism and an aggressive militancy. Unlike the Cathars with which they have been compared, the Paulicians were therefore not in the least pacifistic. Led by former officers of the Byzantine army, Paulicians evangelized with a Crusade-like military fervor, claiming to have been the extension of the original church at Corinth founded by Paul the Apostle. The Paulicians comprised one of the most radical and important heretical

---

[122] Shelley, p. 123.

[123] Bettenson & Maunder, p. 56.

sects of the early medieval period. Having run afoul of the Byzantine Empress Theodora, the Paulicians incurred violent losses of one hundred thousand, revolted under the leadership of a certain Karbeas, built a fortress on the Arab frontier, and, with the help of Moslems, made plundering forays into the Byzantine regions. Predictably, the Paulicians were crushed – not by the overpowering arguments of apologists or the scrutinizing rhetoric of theologians, but by the might and power of a more powerful Greek secular state. Chas Clifton suggests that among their contributions to history, the Paulicians laid the groundwork for the Bogomil heresy that would surface in the tenth century.

A couple of developments need to be mentioned in any history of this sort, though they do not traditionally qualify as heretical: the increasingly pervasive authority of the papacy, and the rise of Eastern Orthodox Christianity. Whereas the Council of Chalcedon could not be expected to end theological disputes forever, it did, along with the earlier Council of Nicea, have the effect of defining orthodoxy and thus pushing dissensions to the fringes. From an official, institutional standpoint, therefore, the church had successfully fought off heresies and secured its highest level of unified orthodoxy.

That seemingly enviable situation could only be bought with a price, however. The church of the early Middle Ages had in the meantime, even if for the commendable purpose of preserving orthodoxy, adopted a glaring heresy in the form of universal papal authority. Through appeals to the centrality of the early Roman church, coupled with an insistence that apostolic authority had been passed along in Rome by a process of historical succession, the bishop of Rome had, by the time of Leo in the fifth and into the sixth century and beyond, come to be widely regarded as the high priest of the empire. The Roman bishop became the *Pontifex Maximus* – the "Head of the Church," the "Vicar of Christ."

Under the rule of the Roman emperor Justinian, the Roman state in the sixth century became virtually indistinguishable from the church. The old tension between church and state, spiritual piety and secular worldliness, vanished completely in the new vision of "Christian society" along the lines of Augustine's conception in *The City of God*. Unsurprisingly, Justinian's claim to unified secular and spiritual power as a Christian emperor – along with his failure to resolve the Monophysite controversy – would help to eventually provoke the Great Schism between East and West, Catholic Rome and Orthodox Constantinople. Moreover, Justinian would come to endorse icons, the identification of physical objects, edifices, images, and flesh-and-bone men with things holy, spiritual, angelic and divine. Idolatry again gripped the church through the veneration of icons and saints. At the same time, as McDowell and Stewart have noted, the schisms occurring within the main arms of Christendom are often overplayed at the expense of a remarkable unity on vital doctrines: "While there is some doctrinal disagreement within the three branches of Christendom – Roman Catholic, Eastern Orthodox and Protestant -- there is a general agreement among them as to the essentials of the faith."[124]

Seventh Century

In an effort to unify and fortify an Eastern Church divided over the issue of Monophysitism, against the rising threat of Islam, Cyrus of Alexandria suggested pulling the opposing sides together through yet another theological formula. A compromise between the dual-natures Christology of Chalcedon and the Monophysite theory advanced by Eutyches, the new formula, as archivists Bettenson and Maunder put it, "admitted the two natures but only one 'divine-human operation or will'."[125] To an opposing party of Duothelites, the Monothelites were merely reasserting the error of Eutyches in regard to not only the nature, but now the will, of Christ. Berkhof adds that their doctrine took two forms: "either the human will was regarded as merged in the divine, or the will was regarded as composite, resulting from the fusion of the divine and the human."[126] This *monothelite* position was published in 638, which resulted in nothing but another schism, which led to another Council, in which the Monothelites were formally condemned by the Emperor, with the backing of the pope.

As the church became immersed in that long, dark era of history known as the Middle Ages, heresies understandably became less common and less conspicuous. Because Christianity had consumed the society of

---

[124] McDowell & Stewart, p. 26.

[125] Bettenson & Maunder, p. 97.

[126] Berkhof, p. 109.

which it had previously been but a part, it took great courage and conscious effort to break away from the inclusiveness of the church. As a result, heresy came to be defined in social and political, as well as doctrinal terms.

A significant Middle Age "counter-cultural" trend, the monastic movement began with notable personalities such as Anthony and Benedict. Irish monasticism, traceable to the missionary work of Patrick in the fifth century, caused considerable headaches for the highly structured, politicized Roman episcopacy. Unlike the heterodox movements that preceded it, this this new Celtic Christianity was especially troublesome because it embraced the same doctrines as Rome. Paul Johnson notes: "Irish monasticism was thus an insidious challenge to the early Dark Age Church and its hold on society. Like the Montanist-type sects, it advocated a return to primitive Christian purity, but unlike them it could not be attacked on grounds of doctrinal error."[127] Though not branded heretics themselves, these intentionally poor and dedicated Irish monks laid the foundation for "heresies" to come, as Rome would eventually denounce vows of poverty and deviations from official Catholic structure and practice as heretical.

Eighth Century

The tradition of venerating Christ, Mary and the saints through the vehicle of icons (images) came to a head in the eighth century. Borrowing moderately dualist concepts from Plato, the icon supporters argued that iconic depictions merely represent on earth the ultimate, eternal realities of heaven. So as Shelley points out, the more philosophical of the *iconodules* (icon sympathizers) held all of the physical realm to be a mere shadow, and eternity the true substance. An opposing party of *iconoclasts* ("idol smashers"), says Shelley, "wanted to replace the religious icons with the traditional Christian symbols of the cross, the Book (Bible), and the elements of the Lord's Supper. These objects alone, they insisted, should be considered holy."[128] Bradley Nassif adds that the iconoclasts "vehemently opposed icons" for three basic reasons: (1) Icons are idols

---

[127] Johnson, p. 144.

[128] Shelley, p. 157.

(as, they felt, Exodus 20:4 made clear); (2) icons are not supported by church tradition, since church fathers such as Origen and Eusebius denounced them; and (3) as strictly physical objects, they deny the hypostatic union (dual-natures) Christology of the Nicene creed.[129] Whittow's description of icons as the basis of superstition bears repeating in full:

> Icons, the images of Christ, the Virgin Mary or the saints, made of mosaic or fresco and covering the walls of churches, or more accessibly painted on wooden panels where they were frequently found in private lay hands, were seen as doors into the spiritual world. Not only were the saints easily recognisable in visions from their images in icons, but the icon itself was regarded as having an intimate relationship with the holy reality it represented. Icons could bleed, sweat, and cry. The scrapings of an icon mixed with...water and drunk as a potion would cure illness.[130]

Ironically, the iconoclasts nonetheless found themselves the heretics. Convened by the stalwart iconodule, the Empress Irene, the seventh Council at Nicea condemned the iconoclastic movement, which, apart from a handful of scattered protestations, never really recovered. Icons remain to this day a major point of division between Eastern and Western versions of Christianity.

Ninth Century

A brilliant but highly ambitious Patriarch of Constantinople, Photius claimed his right to the patriarchate when the sitting Patriarch Ignatius refused communion to the Emperor Bardas and was consequently deposed. Ignatius appealed his right to Pope Nicholas I, who would be bound by law and custom to uphold Ignatius' claim. Evidently sensing the potential

---

[129] Nassif, Bradley, "Kissers and Smashers: Why the Orthodox Killed One Another Over Icons," *Christian History, 16*, 1997.

[130] Mark Whittow, *The Making of Byzantium, 600- 1025* (Berkeley: University of California Press, 1996), p. 139.

for loss of favor among the Greeks, Photius instead built up a case against Rome based on pretexts, such as the papal endorsement of the Frankish kings as rightful emperors of the East, and especially the controversy between Greek and Roman churches over the insertion of the "filioque" ("procession of the Holy Spirit") clause into the Nicean Creed at the Synod of Toledo back in 589.

According to Philip Schaff, "the violent assault of Photius upon the Latin doctrine [of double procession], as heretical, drove the Latin church into the defensive."[131] The "filioque" episode serves as another fine example of hair-splitting trivial dissension at the expense of the testimony of the church and the gospel enterprise. On what turned out to be one of the main causes of the East-West schism, Schaff adds:

> The single word *Filioque* keeps the oldest, largest, and most nearly related churches divided since the ninth century, and still forbids a reunion. The Eastern church regards the doctrine of the single procession as the corner-stone of orthodoxy, and the doctrine of the double procession as the mother of all heresies. She has held most tenaciously to her view since the fourth century, and is not likely ever to give it up. Nor can the Roman church change her doctrine of the double procession without sacrificing the principle of infallibility.[132]

Photius also implicitly denied the supremacy of the pope, a conviction that led to his excommunication by a Roman council in 858. Through various devices Photius thus succeeded in driving a wedge further into the preexisting division between Rome and Constantinople, a schism that would be exploited again by Michael Caerularius in 1054, helping to bring about the larger and more permanent "Great Schism." If causing divisions means heresy (Romans 16:17), then Photius certainly qualifies as a heretic.

A more moderately heterodox figure to emerge from this time was Gottschalk of Orbais, an outspoken monk whose pre-Calvinist views on complete double predestination (that God predestines not only everyone who will be saved, but everyone who will be damned) landed him at the

---

[131] Philip Schaff, *History of the Christian Church, Vol. IV, Medieval Christianity A.D. 500-1073* (New York: Charles Scribner's Sons, 1891), p. 483.

[132] Schaff, *History of the Christian Church, Volume IV*, p. 476

Synod at Mainz, over which presided an old nemesis, Rabanus. To Gottschalk's dismay Rabanus had been promoted to Archbishop, and Rabanus condemned Gottschalk and handed him over, in Schaff's words, "for punishment and safekeeping."

His punishment was severe. By Berkhof's account, Gottschalk was condemned, scourged and sentenced to life imprisonment, all for the keeping of a Semi-Augustinian doctrine remarkably similar to that of his highly orthodox and equally unforgiving critics. His condemnation seems to have resulted from a personal grievance disguised as a theological concern. The *Catholic Encyclopedia* suggests Gottschalk's relative innocence of doctrinal distortions: "It is doubtful whether Gottschalk's doctrine on predestination was heretical. There is nothing in his extant writings that cannot be interpreted in a Catholic sense. He...taught that God does not wish all men to be saved, and that Christ died only for those who were predestined to be saved; but these doctrines are not necessarily heretical."[133]

Tenth Century

One of the first of many dualist "reform" movements to challenge the Roman status quo, Bogomilism actually began in the mid-tenth century, otherwise a conspicuously quiet time for heresies. A Bulgarian priest, Bogomil taught dualism as a matter of genealogy – that God had two sons, Christ and Satanael (Satan). Bogomil and his followers rebuked and rejected the Eastern Orthodox Church as a worldly, fleshly, materialist stronghold of Satanael. As historians such as Chas Clifton have noted, Bogomilism seems to have had a strong political element – in identifying the humble, common believers with the peasantry, and the evil, spiritually corrupt agents of Satan with ecclesiastical and territorial overlords.

Taking the iconoclasts from the eighth century one further, the Bogomils refused to venerate even the cross, as it symbolized the weapon of execution used by Satanael to crucify Christ. Their rigid asceticism involved separation from society, abstinence from meat and wine, and

---

[133] "Gottschalk of Orbais," *The Catholic Encyclopedia, Vol., 6* (New York: Robert Appleton Co., 1909), <http://www.newadvent.org/cathen/06682a.htm. >.

refusing to marry or have children. Bogomilism also appears to have constructed the dualist philosophical foundation upon which Catharism and other emerging heresies could be built. The Bogomils were first publicly rebutted by Cosmas the Priest in his *Sermon Against the Heretics*, around 970 according to Sean Martin. A vigorous and persistent group, they were officially disbanded upon the capture of Constantinople by the Turks in 1453, but a remnant would continue to survive, by some accounts into the nineteenth century.

II. From the Great Schism to the Postmodern Era

Eleventh Century

One uniquely heterodox eleventh century teacher was Roscelin, a monk and philosopher of the Nominalist school. Led by thinkers like Porphyry, and later, William of Occam, Nominalism proposed basically that *universals*, broad abstractions of reality, do not exist in themselves, but are merely words or names (hence *nominalism*) used to designate specific manifestations of reality. Thus individual real entities, like the pope or the blacksmith down the street, can be seen and described in terms of their specific and verifiable attributes, but the abstract category of "popes" or "blacksmiths" cannot be similarly verified and described. Those words are merely terms devised to conceptualize the more concrete reality. Drawing from this way of thinking, Roscelin suggested that the three Personages of the Trinity were of necessity three independent beings. Otherwise, he argued, the Father and the Spirit would be incarnate right along with the Son. The *Catholic Encyclopedia* explains: "He argues that if the three Divine Persons form but one God three have become incarnate, which is inadmissible. There are therefore three Divine substances, three Gods, as there are three angels, because each substance constitutes an individual, which is the fundamental assertion of anti-Realism [nominalism]."[134] So deviant were Roscelin's ideas that he was publicly and effectively refuted not only by the great Scholastic theologian St. Anselm, but even by a fellow freethinker, Peter Abelard.

---

[134] M. De Wulf, "Roscelin," *The Catholic Encyclopedia, Vol. 6* (New York: Robert Appleton Co., 1912), <http://www.newavent.org/>.

Named after the Cathedral at Orléans which served as their home base, the heretics of Orléans were, says Chas Clifton, the first of the Middle Ages groups to be accused of devil worship – along with infant sacrifice, orgies and cannibalism. These outlandish suspicions set an unfortunate precedent that would fuel the Inquisition, along with witch-hunts and various persecutions, for the remainder of church history. One of the notable features of the Orléans heresy was its popularity among all classes – from priests to laypersons.

Like so many heretical groups, the devotees at Orléans were essentially dualist. They also had Manichean tendencies, and were held together by a core of priests. And, again like so many other deviants from orthodoxy, their intentions were not completely demonic. Clifton adds: "Despite the accusations of devil worship and Manichaeism made by some chroniclers at the time, the Orléans heretics appear to have been neither..."[135] Rather, the Orléans heresy evidently had its roots in skeptical intellectualism combined with a sincere desire to reform "what had already become a worldly and too frequently corrupted church." Still, the charge of heresy was not without merit. Under threat of execution before a group of bishops in 1022 at the Temple of Sainte Croix, a group of clerics representing the heretical group admitted to teaching, among other things, that Christ was not born of a virgin, did not suffer on the cross and did not rise from the dead, and that the Scriptures and the sacraments were ultimately worthless symbols of a deeper spiritual life that depended only on the five senses and the guidance of the Holy Spirit. Their confessions did not help them, as they (and their teachings with them) were burned to death a few days later.

Twelfth Century

A standout among heretics, Joachim of Floris (or Flora) was a Benedictine monk whose disciplined studies led him to an imaginative theory of history in which eras of time corresponded to the three persons of the Trinity – the Age of the Father, the Age of the Son, and the Age of the Holy Spirit. The Age of the Father, according to Clifton, was the period of Mosaic law and authority, including the entire range of history preceding

---

[135] Clifton, p. 107.

the advent of Christ. The Age of the Son was the time of Christ, Paul, and the church. Joachim estimated that the Age of the Son would equal the 42 generations from Abraham to Jesus that preceded it, and therefore would also consist of 42 generations, meaning it would end around the year 1260. It would then be followed by the Age of the Holy Spirit, which, after tremendous social upheaval and a brief appearance by the Antichrist, would usher in an unprecedented reign of love and liberty by the Holy Spirit.

Paul Johnson's *History of Christianity* suggests that Joachim's "scientific" teachings on prophecy not only bore influence upon everyone from fellow abbots to Roger Bacon, but seemed almost a spiritual version of Marxism. Joachim was counted a "true prophet" for a time, but then, like most prophets true and false alike, eventually caught the attention of the pope and was condemned. His teachings did continue nonetheless to find a captive audience among Dominican and Franciscan orders in the thirteenth century.

Another loosely defined movement, Catharism first emerged in Northern Europe in the mid twelfth century. Johnson notes that the Cathars were a rather diverse assortment of groups, "also called Publicans, Paterines (in Italy), Bougres or Bulgars in France, or Arians, Manicheans or Marcionites. Around Albi the Cathars were termed Albigensians." Though the names were diverse, as were the ideas, they were alike in embracing a common ideology: "They aimed to substitute a perfect elite for the corrupt clergy." [136]

Chas Clifton therefore proposes that Catharism can be traced all the way back to Novatianism, the first distinct "holier than thou" anti-clerical movement in the church. Catharism was tantamount to a revived Gnosticism. Says Shelley, "Like the Gnostics in the early church, the Cathari held that the universe is the scene of an eternal conflict between two powers, the one good, the other evil. Matter, including the human body, is the work of this evil power, the god of the Old Testament."[137] And, like the Gnostics, the Cathars divided their ranks into distinct levels of spirituality: the "perfect" and the mere "believers." In *The Cathars*, Sean Martin summarizes their influence:

---

[136] Johnson, p. 251.

[137] Shelley, p. 219.

Catharism was the most popular heresy of the Middle Ages. Indeed, such was its success that the Catholic Church and its apologists referred to it as the Great Heresy... The Cathars found widespread support from all areas of society, from kings and counts to carpenters and weavers."[138]

Perhaps their undeniable success making converts explains why the Cathars were the only nominally Christian religious group to have been subjected to an official military Crusade by the church, that being the Albigensian Crusade conducted in the Languedoc region of France beginning in 1208.

Roughly contemporaneous with the Cathars was the movement established by Peter Waldo, a rich merchant-layman from Lyons who became disenchanted with his own prosperity, renounced his worldly possessions and converted to a poor and starkly "apostolic" version of Christianity. Though such a radical act of faith would have been enough to draw suspicion from the church, Waldo bolstered his heretical status by paying some priests to translate the New Testament from Latin to French. Waldo has been charged by church recorders with preaching rebellion against the church, but his primary message had a marked New Testament character – the gospel to the poor.

As might have been expected, Waldo's approach found disfavor with the official church, and he found himself having to file formal petitions for the right to organize and preach. The pope refused, and Waldo, having pondered the example of the apostles in Acts, told his followers, "We must obey God rather than men." They were of course condemned as a result, and sadly caught up in the Inquisition that formed in response to Catharism. Despite full-scale persecution from Rome, the Waldensians managed to thrive throughout Western and Central Europe, even to the present day, drawing on the strength of "the consonance of their practice with their apostolic beliefs." Their example moreover inspired the Hussite and Lollard reform movements to come in the fourteenth and fifteenth centuries.

---

[138] Martin, *The Cathars*.

Thirteenth Century

Some of the more extreme ascetics in church history were the thirteenth century flagellants, so designated for their practice of whipping themselves and their brethren in penance for sin. Though flagellants were initially admired by churchmen for their poverty and self-discipline, the church eventually detected a threat in that the street demonstrations of penance appeared to replace the sacraments provided by the church. Clifton remarks that in the flagellants and related movements (e.g., the Beghards and Beguines) the church was also concerned about two developing "side issues": public displays of penitence undermining private devotion, and the preaching of Jesus's coming devolving into millenarianism.

Francis of Assisi cannot be strictly considered a heretic. In fact, the monastic order originally founded by Francis was endorsed by the pope in 1210. Francis' famous example of poverty and simple faith, however, frequently incurred the suspicions of Rome. As the Franciscan movement gathered steam, it increasingly brought to light the corruption and materialistic excesses of the papal hierarchy. In a sense, living a Christian example became a "heresy," by way of disturbing the conscience of the church. Moreover, as their movement expanded, the Franciscans slowly began to align themselves with openly heretical personalities such as Joachim of Flores. The Franciscans also spawned heretical groups of their own, the "Spirituals." The Spirituals – unlike Francis – criticized the church at large and refused to honor its authority structure. Clifton comments: "Inevitably the issue of Franciscan poverty became a critique of ecclesiastical corruption in general, with the Spirituals accusing the pope, bishops, and abbots of other orders of having strayed too far from the apostolic ideals...."[139] Eventually they evolved into a distinct separatist movement known as the Fraticelli, who in the thirteenth and fourteenth centuries openly denounced the pope and the entire Roman hierarchy. The Franciscan movement as a whole, along with the Waldensians, helped maintain a certain pressure upon the Catholic Church to reform. In 1323, following years of uneasy toleration from Rome, Pope John XXII formally condemned the Franciscan doctrine of absolute poverty as heresy.

---

[139] Clifton, p. 46.

Fourteenth Century

Yet another manifestation of resurrected Gnosticism, the Free Spirit was the appellation given to a number of groups, especially Beguines and Beghards, who according to Clifton "rejected ecclesiastical governance and claimed to perceive God everywhere..." Followers of the Free Spirit movement earned their nickname for their assertions that they had so united their wills with God's that they could do literally whatever they pleased. Moreover, their radically spiritual outlook reflected the old Gnostic tenets of dualism and emanations from the supreme deity. Although they were not officially organized, the Free Spirit adherents were officially condemned by Pope Clement V, with a bull issued in 1311 that summarized the Free Spirit's heretical beliefs. Among those beliefs were, "That someone in this life could reach a state of perfection and be beyond sinning;" "That such a person had such control over his senses that he no longer had to fast or pray;" and the worst one for Rome, "That he is free from all obedience to the church." Though the Free Spirit was definitely a heresy, its severity may have been exaggerated by a church protecting its own interests.

Over the course of centuries, the wealthy institutional church encountered more and more hostility from a poor, cynical but increasingly literate public. The church responded by demonizing and excommunicating its critics as heretics, and thus most "heresies" approaching the time of Luther were merely expressions of protest. Led by the fiercely independent preacher John Wycliffe, the Lollards for example committed themselves to fulfilling a vision of Christianity that included the gospel to all nations and tongues (through Bible translation and preaching), along with renunciation of the Catholic hierarchy as the work of the devil – and the pope its Antichrist.

Like the Waldensians before them, the Lollards went forth "two by two" as poor itinerant preachers to audiences in marketplaces, fields and homes. According to Shelley, Wycliffe himself was so widely admired that the church could not lay a hand on him for fear of a large-scale revolt. His followers were unfortunately not always as well liked, nor as wise. In denouncing not only the church authority system, but the taxes and social policies of the entire civil order, activists in the extreme wing of the Lollards found themselves condemned by church and state alike. They proved resistant to persecution, however, and despite frequent burnings and imprisonments among their members, they maintained a formidable presence in England for the next fifty years. Their uncompromising convictions of Scripture inspired reform movements to follow, notably that of John Hus.

Fifteenth Century

The great Czech reformer John Hus discovered the religious philosophy of Wycliffe while serving as rector and preacher at Bethlehem Chapel near the University of Prague. A graduate of the University, Hus was inspired by the alternative vision of Christianity offered by Wycliffe. Shelley writes that on the walls of the Chapel "were paintings contrasting the behavior of the popes and Christ. The pope rode a horse; Christ walked barefoot. Jesus washed the disciples' feet; the pope preferred to have his kissed."[140] These perceptions were confirmed through readings of Scripture, which became more and more readily available to the public through the efforts of Waldo, Wycliffe, and now Hus himself. According to the *Catholic Encyclopedia*, Hus did not consciously foment a rebellion. Rather, he gradually adopted biblical convictions that stood just outside the norms of the church, such as the "lay chalice," the act of sharing communion openly with the whole body of believers.

When pressed on those convictions, Hus stood by them respectfully but resolutely. For his efforts Hus was tried, condemned and executed at the stake. His legacy refused to die with him, as the flames of persecution merely accelerated his movement with the intensity of wildfire. Hus became a national hero and a symbol of a true, reformed Christian faith. Says Clifton, "Dead, John Hus was a martyr to religious reform and Czech nationalism. Hussite churches were formed, with Bohemians demanding the communion cup and free preaching with the approval of the hierarchy."[141] Shelley notes along similar lines, "The Bohemian rebellion refused to die with Hus."

Among the remnants of the Hussite movement were the two wings of Bohemianism, the moderate Ultraquists and the militant Taborites, named

---

[140] Shelley, p. 240.

[141] Clifton, p. 59.

after Mount Tabor in Scripture. So militant were the Taborites, in fact, that they appointed a military leader, John Trocznowski, also known as Zizka; designed an "armored wagon" that turned out to be a forerunner to the modern tank; and successfully repelled Crusading armies in 1426, 1427 and 1431. Even after enduring serious losses through the ravages of war, an independent remnant of Bohemian-Hussite believers survived, and in 1457 reformed as the United Brethren or Unity of the Brotherhood. Having separated from both Catholics and Ultraquists, the Brethren rallied themselves behind an organized structure—at the top of which sat a council of elders and a presiding judge—and an austere moral code. According to the *Catholic Encyclopedia*, "The strictest morality and modesty were exacted from the faithful. All acts subservient to luxury were forbidden; oaths and military service were only permitted in very exceptional cases. Public sins had to be publicly confessed, and were punished with ecclesiastical penalties or expulsion."[142] Shelley adds that the Brethren "remained a root in dry ground" until the arrival of Luther.

Sixteenth Century

For the papacy in Rome at least, and in terms of long-lasting effects on the organized church, Martin Luther was possibly the greatest of all heretics – a "wild boar" in the vineyard of the Lord, as one papal pronouncement declared. Luther and the leaders of the Protestant Reformation represent the most extreme example of "institutional heresy," that is, heresy defined as non-compliance with church structure and protocol, rather than as deviation from the Word of God. Luther, after all, took his bold stand against the corruption of Rome on the basis of *sola scriptura*, or the principle of sufficient authority in the biblical revelation alone. Contrasting Luther with Erasmus, Johnson assesses the former's character: "not so much an intellect as a great force – a great spiritual force."

Luther's combination of scholarly independence and sincere, childlike faith proved to be a shining example for Calvin, Zwingli, and many

---

[142] Joseph Wilhelm, "Bohemian Brethren," *The Catholic Encyclopedia* (New York: Robert Appleton Company, 1907). <http://www.newadvent.org/cathen/02616a.htm>.

other reformers to come, the kindling that would set the Protestant Reformation ablaze. The Roman Catholic apologist Hilaire Belloc suggests that apart from the influence of Calvin, especially, the arm of Christendom known as "Protestantism" likely would not exist:

> [T]he Protestant movement, which had begun as something merely negative, an indignant revolt against the corruption and worldliness of the official Church, was endowed with a new strength by the creation of Calvinism, twenty years after the upheaval had begun. Though the Lutheran forms of Protestantism covered so great an area, yet the driving power – the centre of vitality – in Protestantism was, after Calvin's book had appeared in 1536, Calvin.[143]

Erasmus, Galileo and Bruno deserve mention if only as noteworthy examples of the growing Renaissance trend toward scientific humanism and individualistic conscientiousness. Much like the slightly more famous reformer to follow him, Martin Luther, Erasmus was converted to an austere, unadorned form of Christian faith through hearing and reading a sound exposition of the book of Romans. Through this process he became captivated by the prospect of personally studying the Scriptures, drawing personal conclusions, and suggesting new interpretations. In that sense, Erasmus represented a new sort of heretic, whose "false teaching" was that science could help inform interpretation of Scripture – and not merely the other way around.

In the case of Erasmus, the plunge into the sciences without a grounding in faith led to abysmal doubt. Galileo took the notion of discovery a bit further, putting the "heretical" heliocentric theory of Copernicus to the empirical test by way of the telescope, and running afoul of the Inquisition as a result. If Daniel Boorstin is correct, Galileo's fate, following the publication of his *Dialogue on the Two Chief World Systems*, was largely the result of external historical circumstances:

> Galileo would be caught in the cross fire between Catholics and Protestants. The rising attacks of Protestantism made it necessary that Pope Urban VII respond by showing the determination of the Church

---

[143] Belloc, *The Great Heresies*.

of Rome to preserve the purity of ancient Christian dogmas. Protestants must have no monopoly on fundamentalism.[144]

Galileo died at the ripe old age of 77 under house arrest in 1642.

The intellectual Bruno, however, entertained such esoteric and clearly non-Christian philosophies that he managed to draw the ire of Catholics and Protestants alike. As the *Catholic Encyclopedia* explains, "Bruno was not condemned for his defence of the Copernican system of astronomy, nor for his doctrine of the plurality of inhabited worlds, but for his theological errors, among which were the following: that Christ was not God but merely an unusually skillful magician, that the Holy Ghost is the soul of the world, that the Devil will be saved, etc."[145] With few friends in high places to support him, Bruno was burned alive as a heretic in 1600.

According to Berkhof, "Socinianism represents a reaction against the Reformation, and in the doctrines of sin and grace it is simply a revival of the old Pelagian heresy."[146] Following the teachings of their rationalist leader, Faustus Socinus, the Socinians embodied the same spirit of certain modern-day liberal-humanist "Christians," who hold that Christianity consists in nothing more than attempting to practice the virtues taught by Christ. Everything else – atonement, justification, the Trinity, the deity of Christ, in some cases even the existence of God – is dispensable. Berkhof again describes Socinians as those who deny original sin and affirm the inherent moral-spiritual "neutrality" of human free will, and therefore repudiate Christianity. "They need no Savior nor any extraordinary interposition of God to secure their salvation." Various historians have recognized connections between Socinianism and the later phenomenon of Unitarianism.

---

[144] Daniel Boorstin, *The Discoverers* (New York: Vintage, 1985), p. 325.

[145] William Turner, "Giordano Bruno," *Catholic Encyclopedia* (New York: Robert Appleton Company, 1908). <http://www.newadvent.org/cathen/ 03016a.htm>.

[146] Berkhof, p. 149.

Seventeenth Century

In 1603, a Dutch Professor of Divinity named Jacob Arminius charged that Calvinism – specifically the doctrine of predestination – made God the author of sin. Unfortunately, such an inflammatory suggestion resulted in the banishment of the Arminians ("Remonstrants") from the Reformed Church in 1618 by a synod at Dort, leaving their more intriguing issues unsettled. Arminians argued as case in point that whereas grace is universal, it might not be "irresistible." To the contrary, grace may on occasion be abused or rejected. Similarly, faith derives not only from God's grace, but from the human will to accept it. Thus the first of the Five Articles of the Remonstrants' states:

> 1. That God, by an eternal and unchangeable purpose in Jesus Christ, his Son, before the foundations of the world were laid, determined to save, out of the human race which had fallen into sin, in Christ, for Christ's sake and through Christ, those who through the grace of the Holy Spirit shall believe...[147]

In accommodating human volition, this modified view of grace became a lasting feature of the Christian church. Even Reformed theologians like R.C. Sproul concede that the *prescient* view of predestination, that God in foreknowledge chooses those who will choose Him, is held by the "vast majority of Christians." Most historians of church doctrine (e.g., Berkhof) nonetheless associate Arminianism with Pelagianism or Semi-Pelagianism. Among other historical legacies, the division of Methodism into the Wesley-Arminian and the Whitefield-Calvinist camps has been attributed to Arminianism.

Between the Reformers and the traditional papal hierarchy of the seventeenth century arose a bishop, Cornelius Jansen, who was, in Paul Johnson's words, "a Catholic Lutheran." Jansen stood against the political-mindedness of the Jesuit canon law, the spiritual corruption of the papacy, and the secular corruption of the monarchy. "The Jansenists," says

---

[147] Bettenson & Maunder, p. 271.

Johnson, "were the Manichees of the pre-Enlightenment, the first harbingers of modern philosophies of pessimism."[148] By an emphasis on the Augustinian doctrines of original sin, human depravity, and divinely appointed predestination, Jansenism also closely mirrored the more recently developed doctrines of Calvin, and probably struck too close to Protestantism for Rome to abide. Jansen's writings were anathemized by orthodox theologians and the pope himself, but found receptive audiences in sensitive, reflective thinkers like Blaise Pascal. As a middle ground position between faith and reason, Pascal's philosophy likewise failed to make any mark on the established church, but did help open the door to the Enlightenment to come.

Eighteenth Century

As Renaissance learning advanced, still under the auspices of a Christian society, it slowly evolved into Enlightenment – a thoroughgoing philosophical rethink of history, science and epistemology, often culminating in a complete disconnect with Christianity. Thus the Enlightenment spawned skeptics like David Hume, deist social critics such as Diderot and Voltaire, pantheists like Spinoza, and a few outright atheists, Baron d'Holbach for one example. Their efforts opened a virtual Pandora's Box of unbelief to an inquisitive modern society, a box that has never again been shut. The Enlightenment also featured a distinct political element, motivating thinkers as diverse as Locke and Rousseau to launch critiques of the secular monarchy right along with papal authority and the official Scholastic theology originally devised by St. Thomas Aquinas. The result was an unprecedented break in the entire system of "Christendom." As Shelley says, "The Middle Ages and the Reformation were centuries of faith in the sense that reason served faith, the mind obeyed authority. To a Catholic it was church authority, to a Protestant biblical authority, but in either case God's Word came first, not man's thoughts…. The Age of Reason rejected that."[149] It turns out that the seeds of humanism, which would

---

[148] Johnson, p. 347.

[149] Shelley, p. 324.

bear so much unbelieving fruit in the twentieth century, were actually sown back in the eighteenth.

The eighteenth century therefore brought with it a new and irreverent approach to biblical studies, notably in the resurrection-as-hoax theory suggested by H. S. Reimarus and published by Gotthold Lessing. These new critical thinkers and their methods anticipated the famous "Quest" for the historical Jesus to be undertaken by scholars such as Schweitzer in the nineteenth century, and even the "Jesus myth" and "Da Vinci Code" theories still floating around in the twenty-first. The Enlightenment led most educated people to dismiss or trivialize accounts of the miraculous as religious fabrications. It could be argued that the real scandal of Enlightenment was an unwarranted yet wholesale rejection of history, hence of the very foundations of Christian belief. As Colin Brown summarized the teaching of Kant, "No generation should be bound by the creeds and dogmas of previous generations."[150]

Freemasonry and the Masons make for one of the more elusive, ill-defined and esoteric heretical sects in history. The strange movement was "officially" born in 1717, by most accounts, at a gathering of Craft Lodges at a tavern in London. Regardless, says John L. Brooke, "The origins and growth of Freemasonry and the explosion of a revived religious occult in the late eighteenth century are topics of immense complexity."[151] Despite established connections with Gnosticism, millenarianism, Enlightenment rationalism and deism, alchemy and the mystery religions, Freemasonry survived largely by associating itself with a mystical kind of Christian faith. Among the false doctrines embraced by the Masons was, says Brooke, a belief in "the restoration of the paradisial powers of Adam," with the rites of Freemasonry "paving" the road to perfection. This and other obscure, elitist doctrines appealed to certain believers, foremost among them Joseph Smith, the founder of Mormonism. According to Dominguez and others, Freemasonry has been banned or condemned by the Catholic Church, as well as by numerous Protestant denominations,

---

[150] Colin Brown, *Philosophy and the Christian Faith* (Downer's Grove, IL: Intervarsity, 1968), p. 91.

[151] John L. Brooke, *The Refiner's Fire: The Making of Mormon Cosmology, 1644-1844* (New York: Cambridge University Press, 1994) p. 94.

including Baptists, Presbyterians, Methodists, and even the Russian Orthodox Church. Clearly Freemasonry cannot be reconciled with the Christian faith.

Nineteenth Century

From the Enlightenment breeding on the European continent, a number of religious heresies were introduced, particularly in America. Increasingly well-educated Americans found "traditional" Christianity distasteful, and migrated toward an intellectually respectable version known as Unitarianism. With their "base of operations" at Harvard University, well known Unitarians included Henry Adams, John Quincy Adams and Oliver Wendell Holmes. According to Johnson, Unitarianism could actually be traced to the days of the freethinking reformer Erasmus, and in theological terms to Arius in the fourth century. Clearly it was sanctioned and empowered by the Enlightenment.

Like Arianism, Unitarianism rejects the idea of Trinity, and in keeping with Enlightenment principles, promotes reason above revelation. Says the *Columbia Encyclopedia*, "Originally a scripturally oriented movement, in the mid-19th cent. Unitarianism became a religion of reason under the leadership of James Martineau in England and Ralph Waldo Emerson and Theodore Parker in the United States."[152] Most New England communities were somewhat divided among Unitarians and Congregationalists, whose modern-day counterparts are liberal humanists and conservative Christians. Unitarianism was, and still is, marked by a curious duplicity: a professing love for all mankind, combined with a rather parochial intellectual snobbery. As Johnson recounts, "critics joked that its preaching was limited to 'the fatherhood of God, the brotherhood of man and the neighborhood of Boston.'" Because they embrace a doctrine of universal salvation for all, Unitarians are also known as "Unitarian Universalists."

---

[152] "Unitarianism," *The Columbia Encyclopedia*, 6th ed. <http://www.encyclopedia.com/philosophy-and-religion/christianity/protestant-denominations/unitarians.>.

Joseph Smith's weird journey into false doctrine began with personal "visions" and revelations, some of which would constitute material for his books and doctrines. In 1829 Smith unveiled his new religion, one which – like so many heresies before and since – purported to embody a restored "primitive apostolic church." The new books of revelations introduced by Smith boasted authority equal to that of Moses and Christ. Moreover, the revelations had been allegedly copied directly from gold plates, discovered by Smith on a hill in Manchester, New York, following a personal visitation from an angel.

Mormonism thus featured its own prophets, its own sacred writings, and its own institutional church. In fact, his Mormon church, or the Church of Jesus Christ of Latter-Day Saints, was intended to ultimately displace all other religions as the one, true faith. McDowell and Stewart say, "The claims of Joseph Smith and his followers are clear. The Church of Jesus Christ of Latter-Day Saints claims it is God's true church on earth while all others are wrong."[153] Other claims include an assertion that the Bible cannot be translated correctly, because the Catholic church took it over and corrupted it – therefore, revelation from God now depends entirely on a "true prophet," i.e., Joseph Smith, or his successor, Brigham Young, or the currently presiding leader of the church, the "living prophet." Mormonism also radically distorts Christian theology and anthropology, to say that God was formerly a man, and that man is destined to become a god. Smith himself intoned,

"As Man is, God was,
"As God is, Man may become."

Led by Christian apologists like Walter Martin and Hank Hanegraaff, the Evangelical church at large has rejected the bizarre and exclusivist doctrines of Mormonism, identifying their religious system as a cult.

In 1875, Mary Baker Eddy published her "principles" of spirituality, healing and metaphysics in a book entitled *Science and Health* (to which was later added the *Key to the Scriptures* in 1883). Among Ms. Eddy's more disturbing claims were her presumed status as a prophetess equal to the Apostle Paul in authority, her claim to have restored the healing power

---

[153] McDowell & Stewart, *Handbook of Today's Religions*, p. 66.

of Jesus that had been inactive since the days of the Apostles, and the appeal to her own writings as divine revelation. Like Gnosticism and so many other false teachings before and since, Christian Science maintains a firm distinction between "Jesus" and "the Christ," even going so far as to assert, "Jesus is not God." Christian Science glibly dismisses the physical realm and the evil that pervades it as illusory or unreal.

As any Christian college student today would attest, Darwin's theory of evolution had as much to do with theology as biology or geology, and eventually emerged as possibly the most pervasive false doctrine of the twentieth century. Published famously in 1859 in a race to the presses with Alfred Wallace's own evolutionary theory, Darwin's *On the Origin of Species* found a receptive audience among a freethinking nineteenth century public disenchanted with traditional Victorian religious moralism. For his part, however, Darwin was inspired to construct his theory not only on the basis of observations of nature, but for largely pessimistic, philosophical reasons. Ernst Mayr notes that the death of Darwin's ten-year-old daughter, Annie, "seems to have extinguished the last traces of theism in Darwin."[154] If nothing else, the historical evidence of Darwin's theological disillusionment should help debunk the modern myth that scientists are guided only by an objective methodology based on facts.

Darwin directly inspired the "creative evolution" of Herbert Spencer, along with Marx's historical doctrine of progress through struggle, and a host of pseudo-Christian, New Age belief systems involving "spiritual evolution." Hunt and McMahon have noted perceptively:

> Perhaps no other idea within the last few centuries has had more impact upon twentieth-century mankind than the theory of evolution. It has directly or indirectly influenced nearly every aspect of our modern culture. Evolution was an established religious belief at the heart of occultism and mysticism thousands of years before the Greeks gave it 'scientific' status.[155]

---

[154] Ernst Mayr, *One Long Argument: Charles Darwin and the Genesis of Modern Evolutionary Thought* (Cambridge, MA: Harvard University Press, 1991), p. 15.

[155] Dave Hunt & T.A. McMahon, *The New Spirituality* (Eugene, OR:

But its theological implications are what make Darwinism stand out historically. As taught in textbooks, Darwinism openly repudiates the doctrine of creation, with predictable effects on the spiritual atmosphere: "Over the last two or three centuries, science has become almost completely disconnected from its biblical roots, with the result that the academic culture in which science is practiced today is one of tacit – if not explicit – atheism."[156] Nonetheless, Christian students and intellectuals to this day have attempted to fuse the book of Genesis with the *Origin*, usually choosing to allegorize or otherwise water down Genesis rather than risk reproach from their peers by questioning or criticizing Darwin's politically and emotionally charged theory.

"As serious as the challenge of science was to orthodox Christianity," says Bruce Shelley, "it was clearly secondary to the new views of history."[157] One of the popular conclusions to come out of the higher-critical school was the belief that Moses did not in fact write the first five books of the Bible, or the Pentateuch. Rather, the "Documentary Hypothesis" proposed by Julius Wellhausen suggested that the Pentateuch was the product of various writers representing various phases of Israel's formation and history. Through the imaginative efforts of scholars like David Strauss and Ernest Renan, New Testament studies fared no better. The life of the "historical Jesus" was mapped out as that of a deluded if charismatic prophet whose politically disturbing message led to his tragic execution.

Twentieth Century

Around the turn of the twentieth century, 1906 to be exact, the Pentecostal movement officially began at Azusa Street in Los Angeles. After three years of revival – in the form of thousands receiving the baptism of the Holy Spirit, "with the evidence of speaking in tongues" – new Pentecostal denominations began to spring up around the U.S. These included

---

Harvest House, 1988), p. 220.

[156] Paul Garner, *The New Creationism: Building Scientific Theories on a Biblical Foundation* (Carlisle, PA: Evangelical Press, 2009), p. 13.

[157] Shelley, p. 415.

the Assemblies of God, the Church of God, the Church of God in Christ, and the Pentecostal Holiness Church. Some sixty years later, a "Charismatic Renewal" began in the church at large, with believers from every major denomination having (or claiming) spiritual experiences of tongues, prophecy, and other gifts of the Spirit. Even Roman Catholicism sanctioned the movement within its ranks.

Pentecostals have proven highly evangelistic, effectively spreading their fire to Latin America and other regions. Their commendable emphasis on spiritual power and preaching to the poor and disenfranchised have doubtless contributed to their successes. At the same time, Pentecostalism frequently manifests a heretical underside. (I write this as a Pentecostal.) Much like the Gnostics and so many other dualist heretics, Pentecostals often draw overly sharp divisions between flesh and spirit, in everything from books, music and movies to dress. In many Pentecostal camps, speaking in tongues is used as a litmus test of spirituality (or even of salvation), a means of discriminating between "Spirit filled" and lesser, ordinary mortals. At the top of many Pentecostal spiritual hierarchies are the leaders, those "anointed ones," like Oral Roberts or Jimmy Swaggart, who speak prophetically to the church. Because these leaders are deemed more "spiritual" than ordinary believers, they often feel free to commit sins in the flesh, such as fornication, while claiming to still love God "in the Spirit."

Theologians and scholars such as F. N. Lee have argued that in its emphasis on spiritual gifts and experiences at the expense of sound teaching, Pentecostalism also seems to have connections with the ancient heresies of Montanism and antinomianism. Says Lee, "Pentecostalism is essentially antinomian... It is ebullient, ecstatic, effervescent, and ephemeral entertainment."[158] Many of the aberrant splinter groups and movements that formed in the twentieth century, particularly in America, are Pentecostal in origin. These include The Way International, The Latter Rain movement led by William Branham, Oneness Pentecostalism, and more recently, the Brownsville and Toronto Charismatic revivals. The

---

[158] Francis N. Lee, *Pentecostalism: New Outpouring – Or Ancient Heresy?*, <http://www.francisnigellee.com/wp-content/uploads/2014/02/ Pentecostalism-New-Outpouring-or-Ancient-Heresy-Dr.-F.N.-Lee.pdf.>

materialistic excesses of the "Word-Faith" (or "Positive Confession") movement are likewise traceable in part to classical Pentecostalism.

The twentieth century was undoubtedly the century of the cult. Though clearly non-Christian, cults do often make Christian professions and lay claim to biblical revelations. Cults are hard to define, but may be best understood through the perspective of the follower, who according to sociologist Jean-Marie Abgrall, "weds himself to the doctrines of the cult, is effectively submissive to the guru and gradually cuts himself off from the rest of the world."[159] Through this process a dependency is created, which is fed through the rules, rites and rituals of the organization, all of which serve to "dissolve the individual into the group." Some of the more notorious and wildly deviant cults include the Boston movement or Boston Church of Christ, the Branch Davidians (led by David Koresh), The Way International, The Worldwide Church of God, The Children of God, Erhard Seminars Training (EST), Heaven's Gate, the People's Temple (Jim Jones), the Church of Scientology, the Watchtower Bible and Tract Society (or Jehovah's Witnesses), and the Unification Church of Rev. Sun Myung Moon. The common denominator in this otherwise diverse set of cults is a set of heretical teachings promulgated and enforced through the leadership of a single dominant, if charismatic, personality.

Another twentieth century cult – and not even nearly the largest – deserves some space of its own simply for vividly demonstrating the cyclical persistence of heresies. Nearly 2,000 years after the Gnostics appeared and disappeared from the stage of church history, the Unity School of Christianity virtually mirrors every ancient Gnostic doctrine in detail. For good reason, McDowell and Stewart declare plainly that "The basic world view of Unity is that of Gnosticism."[160] Unity is dualist, as is Gnosticism, regarding matter as an evil. The God of Unity, like the supreme deity of Gnosticism, cannot be known personally, but only apprehended intellectually, as a revelation of the divine mystery or "principle" of love. And like the Gnostics, adherents of the Unity school regard Jesus and "the Christ" as separate entities –which helps explain why the

---

[159] Jean-Marie Abgrall, *Soul Snatchers: The Mechanics of Cults* (New York: Algora, 2000), p. 10-11.

[160] McDowell & Stewart, *Handbook of Today's Religions*, p. 132.

Unity theory of atonement depends on reincarnation rather than faith in Jesus Christ. Unity moreover, and in seeming contradiction with its own philosophical dualism, encourages the attainment of health and wealth through the proper exercise of faith. Founder Charles Fillmore openly sported his greed as a virtue. Unity therefore has much in common with Word-Faith theology, as Hank Hanegraaff and others have observed.

One of the many outcroppings of the rebellion of the youth against the "establishment" during the turbulent sixties, the humanistic *New Age* movement has proven a lasting feature of the American social landscape. Hunt and McMahon have extensively documented "the fact that millions of people are now being trained to contact 'spirit (or inner) guides' through such proliferating Eastern meditation techniques as transcendental meditation, and mind dynamics courses such as Silva Mind Control."[161] These various techniques could be categorized under the broad heading of sorcery or Shamanism, but it could all be described as New Age. Astrology, fortune telling, channeling, holistic healing, séances, and other ancient "New Age" religious practices represent a dangerous heresy, in that Christians have imported them into the church with an alarmingly casual acceptance. Evidently, New Age occult spirituality has found a place in the church for no other reason than that "it works." Perhaps it does work. McDowell and Stewart concede, "There is a reality in the occultic experience which attracts many people to it. All of us desire some sort of ultimate answer for life's basic questions, and the world of the occult gladly supplies answers."[162] Understanding that reality for what it is, Christians would be advised to recall that Satan enjoys a measure of spiritual power himself, and frequently poses as "an angel of light" (2 Cor. 11:14).

Also known as the "faith movement," or the "positive confession" movement, Word-Faith teachings derive largely from Gnosticism, and bear clear similarities to the aforementioned Unity and Christian Science schools, and even classical Pentecostalism. According to Hank Hanegraaff, popular Word-Faith leaders Kenneth Hagin and Kenneth

---

[161] Hunt & McMahon, p. 18.

[162] McDowell & Stewart, p. 157.

Copeland both unashamedly attribute the success of their ministry to Pentecostal evangelists such as T. L. Osborn and William Branham. Other Word-Faithers have drawn inspiration from the likes of Oral Roberts and A.A. Allen, whose personal behavior sapped their credibility in most other quarters of Christianity. However, as Hanegraaff points out, the theology of these faith teachers can be traced almost unfailingly to the works of E.W. Kenyon, "who represents the genesis of the modern-day Word of Faith movement."[163]

A cult leader of sorts himself, Kenyon advocated a neo-Gnostic theology that divides flesh and spirit in dualistic metaphysical terms, arranges believers along a hierarchy of presumed spirituality, and promotes a special, supernatural "revelation knowledge" above the "sense knowledge" common to most ordinary believers. Like the second century heretic Marcion, Kenyon also expressed disdain for the Old Testament, and favored the letters of Paul as spiritually superior to the writings of the other Apostles. A prominent example of Word-Faith leadership, Kenneth Copeland teaches that faith is a "spiritual force" that can be harnessed to gain wealth; that God and men ("little gods") are virtually indistinguishable; and that God's covenants represent financial contracts rather than interpersonal relationships.

Following the tradition of Schweitzer's "Quest for the Historical Jesus," scholars in the twentieth century began excursions into form criticism, source criticism and more "quests." Of these scholars, Rudolf Bultmann may have been the most perniciously influential. Bultmann asserted that a substantial majority of New Testaments texts and traditions were mythological in nature. To find the real Jesus of history, said Bultmann, it is necessary to strip the Gospels and letters of their mythical – i.e. spiritual or supernatural – content. Following Bultmann, Paul Tillich expanded upon the former's personalized, existential approach to faith. For Tillich, God was the "ground of being," the Deity who must be believed in if life is to hold any meaning. This should not be confused with an evangelistic appeal to salvation; Tillich's theology can be reduced to pretty much whatever one would prefer it to be.

In more recent years New Testament "scholarship" produced the Jesus Seminar, a series of studies by radical critics that led to some strikingly

---

[163] Hank Hanegraaff, *Christianity in Crisis* (Nashville: Thomas Nelson, 2009), p. 17.

heretical conclusions – for instance that Jesus did not utter the majority of sayings attributed to Him, that Jesus did not rise from the dead, and that perhaps Jesus never existed at all. Amazingly, many Christians accept these assertions, concluding that their faith resides ultimately in the teachings and the spirit of Jesus, not the historical genuineness of His birth, teaching and miracles, or His death and resurrection. This all amounts to a modern declaration of Docetism, and a reminder of just how far unbelief will stray into the irrational.

Twenty-First Century Outlook

By the end of the twentieth century, the church in its dealings with heretics had come full circle. The most destructive and deceptive of heresies from the first centuries had resurrected, seemingly with even more power than before. Twenty-first century Christians are therefore still called to combat heresies, because the same legalism, Gnosticism, dualism, antinomianism, Docetism and charismatic excess that caused so much doubt and division in the early church are still thriving today. Some of the newer developments in the church that bear examination in this context include the liberal Emergent Church movement led by Brian McLaren, and the tendency toward excess at the expense of doctrine in the Charismatic revivals, such as the Toronto and Brownsville movements dating from the mid-nineties. Paul's ancient counsel to Timothy proves equally pertinent today: "Preach the word! Be ready in season and out of season. Convince, rebuke, exhort, with all longsuffering and teaching. For the time will come when they will not endure sound doctrine..." (2 Tim. 4:1-2). Until the time that no one is left to hear, our calling from God remains, to counter falsehoods by declaring the truth of the gospel faithfully.

10. The Human Condition and the Hope of the Gospel

Towards the end of *The Matrix Reloaded,* the second of the classic Matrix movie trilogy, is a fascinating scene in which the prophesied liberator of the human race, Neo, confronts the Architect, the creator of the Matrix.[164] As laid out in the first movie, the Matrix is an elaborate computer simulation which captive humans are "plugged into" from birth to keep them from rebelling against the ruling system. While continually distracted by the living of their lives, so to speak, in the Matrix, humans provide an unending energy source for machines, which have become self-aware and have taken over the world. Neo is one of a handful who have been "unplugged" and are now in the "real world" leading a resistance. When Neo finally arrives at the Source of the Matrix, the machine mainframe, he faces the Architect, himself a machine who speaks with godlike authority and precision. The Architect explains why the Matrix has been intentionally redesigned with its numerous and transparent flaws:

> The first matrix I designed was quite naturally perfect. It was a work of art, flawless, sublime. A triumph equaled only by its monumental failure. The inevitability of its doom is as apparent to me now as a consequence of the imperfection inherent in every human being; thus I redesigned it based on your history to more accurately reflect the varying grotesqueries of your nature. However, I was again frustrated by failure. I have since come to understand that the answer eluded me because it required a lesser mind, or perhaps a mind less bound by the parameters of perfection.

As the Architect's speech suggests, human beings do not seem comfortable with the idea of a perfect existence, because perfection entails a lack of freedom to be, well, imperfect. History's long record of rebellions and revolutions indicates that many, if not most, people value freedom more highly than even their own health and happiness. But could there exist a

---

[164] *The Matrix Reloaded*, written and directed by the Wachowski Brothers, Warner Bros. Pictures (2003).

world in which decisions borne of genuine freedom culminate in everlasting joy? As a Christian theist I would answer in the affirmative. I suggest that Christian theology best explains humanity's strongest psychological inclinations, two especially:

1. The universal human awareness of evil and experience of suffering is evidence of the fall of man, the violation of God's transcendent moral law through the abuse of free will.

2. The universal human longing for absolute happiness is evidence of the hope of eternal life, to be ultimately realized in the kingdom of heaven through the exercise of faith.

Evil and the Fall of Man

If the first proposition is correct, it may be premature for philosophers to argue that evil – even so-called "gratuitous evil" – is incompatible with theism, because Christian theism in particular explicitly posits the emergence of evil into the world through human transgression against the commandment of God. On this account even the worst and seemingly most pointless suffering ultimately derives from sin, a willful abuse of moral freedom in the presence of a morally pure (holy) God. This "free will defense," first proposed by Augustine and later developed in detail by Christian philosopher Alvin Plantinga, depends on the supposition that the freedom to do good and evil is better, all things considered, then no moral freedom at all. Thus God was good to "give" us free will.

But of course the intrinsic goodness of creating sentient beings capable of great moral responsibility (hence great evil as well as great good) is not self-evident for everyone. Anticipating the skepticism of the later Enlightenment, the seventeenth century French philosopher Pierre Bayle, for example, argued:

The free-will of the first man, which preserved in him sound and entire, in the circumstances wherein he was to make use of it to his own loss, to the ruin of mankind, to the eternal damnation of the greatest part of his posterity, and to the introduction of a terrible deluge of evils, of guilt, and punishment, was not a good gift.[165]

Atheists ever since have been known to contend not only that Christian faith is "wishful thinking," but that the very world which Christians believe God to have created is loaded with (seemingly, at least) gratuitous evils.[166] But that position follows neither from an understanding of Christian theology nor from what it means for something to be evil. Given that the Christian God exists, Christian theology is clearly not wishful thinking, precisely *because* we live in a sinful, fallen world scarred throughout by the painfully stark reality of evil and suffering. In other words theology offers a viable *explanation* for evil, and not merely an arbitrarily devised fantasy of one day escaping it. The hope of eternal life makes sense theologically, if only because it rationally counteracts the emergence of evil, which itself only seems to make sense in a theological context.

On the other hand, on the premise that no transcendent source of moral rules (i.e., God) exists, there is no real "evil" to speak of, gratuitous or otherwise (beyond emotional responses to suffering within a morally indifferent universe). There may exist certain realities which cause pain to us, and we may cause pain to one another, but on the view that we are highly evolved primates struggling for survival in a naturalistic universe, there is nothing inherently evil about pain, whatever form its causes may take. As I wrote in an earlier book, "If nature is really all that exists or all that can be experienced, as naturalism implies, then it seems there should be no objective morality; hence no good or evil, hence no evil."[167] Thus there is a real problem of evil that confronts naturalistic atheism.

---

[165] Pierre Bayle, *An Historical and Critical Dictionary* (London: Hunt and Clarke, 1826), p. 66.

[166] My personal view is that "gratuitous evil" is redundant. If the perceived evil of suffering is not gratuitous, but rather appropriately distributed (like a punishment that fits the crime), then it isn't evil. Only if suffering is gratuitous in the first place can it really be evil. Even then, Christian theology makes clear that all evil and injustice (gratuitous suffering included) will be eternally remedied in righteous judgment at the throne of God.

[167] McIntosh, *Transcending Proof*, p. 16.

Given that there is such a thing as moral *being*, or "objective moral values" as William Lane Craig says, this reality of good and evil calls for an explanation. Naturalistic evolution offers one explanation – collective survival instinct – for why there might *appear* to be something like a moral reality independent of particular human opinions. But moral intuition borne of evolving survival instincts is merely a by-product or epiphenomenon of evolution, more shadow than substance. To be sure, if it's true that virtually anything can be justified in the name of "survival," as seems to be the case, then evolution permits any and all behaviors whatsoever, no matter how widely at variance with our traditional moral understandings. If there is in fact an ontological moral reality, a something called "morality," it would not seem to have much to do with evolutionary naturalism.

Christian theists like C.S. Lewis and William Lane Craig have often argued that the reality of evil actually suggests theism. That is, evil implies an intelligently and transcendently derived moral law, which in turn implies an intelligent and transcendent moral legislator – presumably God. Some skeptics have countered, however, that even if the law of good and evil suggests a deity, it suggests only a deeply *flawed* deity, one who at best allows evil and at worst actively promotes it. With just such a premise in mind, philosopher Stephen Law has advanced what he calls the "evil-god challenge." According to the evil-god hypothesis, as Law terms it, there exists a creator of the universe, and moreover this creator is omnipotent and omniscient. Unfortunately that's where this god's similarity to the God of Christian theism ends:

> But suppose he is not maximally good. Rather, imagine that he is maximally evil. His depravity is without limit. His cruelty knows no bounds. There is no other god or gods – just this supremely wicked being. Call this the evil-god hypothesis.[168]

Law goes on to defend the evil-god hypothesis against one potential defeater, the *problem of good*, or "why an omnipotent, omniscient, and supremely evil being would allow quite so much good into his creation."

---

[168] Stephen Law, "The evil-god challenge," *Religious Studies*, 46 (New York: Cambridge University Press, 2010), p. 356.

What makes the evil-god challenge so interesting is that for every theodicy proposed for the God of traditional theism against the problem of evil there is, or appears to be, an exactly corresponding counter-theodicy that can be proposed to defend evil-god against the problem of good. Against the soul-making theodicy of Hick, in which God uses hardship and loss to build the spiritual character of people so they can more deeply appreciate goodness, Law suggests that evil-god allows love and beauty only in order to accentuate hate and ugliness, so that sufferers can learn to more deeply despise the evil they experience. Just a few really wealthy, powerful (and so presumably happy) people are needed "to make the suffering of the rest of us even more acute." Law's point seems to be that all the vagaries of our moral universe permit rational interpretations not just theistic and atheistic but downright diabolical.

I suggest there is a way to break Law's rhetorical impasse, namely with an appeal to the ontology of goodness itself, as expressed in Augustine's observation that evil is (must be) *privation of good*. On this view evil is little more than the absence of good, a corruption of what God has made. Thus a hateful, cruel and lazy man is also loveless, merciless and shiftless, whereas it would make no sense to say that a loving, merciful and diligent man is hate-less, cruelty-less and laziness-less. Love, mercy and diligence are positive moral attributes; hate, cruelty and laziness the negative attributes ascribed to those who fail them. This makes sense of Paul's statement that "all have sinned [committed evil acts] and [thereby] *fall short* of the glory of God" (Rom. 3:23). Our ongoing experiences of evil in the world serve as constant reminders of the fact that man has sinned against his God by falling short of God's righteousness. Even the atheist philosopher Schopenhauer recognized that the very notion of moral perfection, of innate righteousness, points to the fall of Adam:

> Why the will erred, how it erred, how it could have erred, Schopenhauer does not say, and knows he cannot say – they are questions beyond all power of answer. But the idea of a fall... seemed to him a metaphysical and a moral necessity.[169]

---

[169] Salter, William M., "Schopenhauer's Contact with Theology," *Harvard Theological Review*, Vol. 4, No. 3 (1911), p. 290.

Following the ancient philosopher Epicurus, most of us at one time or another have asked, "Whence comes evil?" (We ask it whenever we find someone committing an act of overt wickedness and cry out in exasperation, "What's *wrong* with that person?") I propose that any acceptable answer to that question must begin with an acknowledgment that evil is not a *thing* to be examined or analyzed, but the practical, spiritually significant outcome of failing God's righteousness. But if God is perfectly good, and the supervisor of a perfectly good creation, it might still be reasonably asked how anyone could fail God's righteousness in the first place.

My own answer begins with the historical-theological observation that God, as narrated in Genesis, at creation conferred great dignity upon human beings by giving them (us) not only wide-ranging moral freedom but tremendous responsibility to manage the affairs of the world we inhabit. Richard Swinburne alludes to this with his "argument from providence." The basic idea is that freedom is a great good. Human beings are baffled by evil (and attribute it to a failure of God) because we neither understand nor appreciate the power we have to influence the moral direction of the world.

Consider the "Song of the Vineyard" in Isaiah 5, a parable speaking metaphorically of God's care and provision for his people:

> My Well-beloved has a vineyard on a very fruitful hill.
> He dug it up and cleared out its stones,
> And planted it with the choicest vine.
> He built a tower in its midst,
> And also made a winepress in it;
> So he expected it to bring forth good grapes,
> But it brought forth wild grapes (Isaiah 5:1-2).

This "vineyard" alludes further to the Garden of Eden, where the first couple was given great provision and every reason to prosper under the watch of their creator. But they were also morally free, and therefore able to disobey as well as obey their Lord by eating of the one forbidden tree. Thus God asks his rebellious people, the "wild grapes" of his vineyard: "...O inhabitants of Jerusalem and men of Judah... What more could have been done to my vineyard that I have not done in it? Why, then, when I expected it to bring forth good grapes, did it bring forth wild grapes?" (v.

3-4). God being omniscient, the question is obviously rhetorical. We may call this the "good God challenge." The point seems to be that pains and problems may arise in the vineyard, no matter how well-tended, from within the "grapes" themselves. Here God almost appears to "isolate the variable" of free will in the hearts of his people, to underscore the truth that the human heart is the one variable that divine providence cannot – or more properly, will not – directly control.

All this seems consistent not only with Christian theology, but with observations of the world around us. Evil does not derive from an evil god, but from the corrupted hearts of morally free human beings who have, in their turn, been tempted by Satan (himself a corrupted being as thoroughly evil as one can be, hence as close to Law's "evil-god" as one can be).

Desire and Dissatisfaction

However, even if an academic problem of evil (whether logical or evidential) were to be finally "solved" to the satisfaction of all interested parties, evil would presumably still be a very real, very painful problem that would continue to menace humanity. Yet for all that, humanity continues to hope for something better. In fact, at any given time most of us are hoping for something much, much better than the often boring or painful set of circumstances currently facing us. Likewise, despite a lifetime of things not generally going our way, most of us still get seriously agitated whenever things don't go our way. "We behave," say Kreeft and Tacelli, "as if we remember Eden and can't recapture it, like kings and queens dressed in rags who are wandering the world in search of their thrones."[170] For C.S. Lewis, these restless agitations and pangs of intense longing are evidence of an exceedingly greater eternal reality held out for us by God: "If I find in myself a desire which no experience in this world can satisfy, the most probable explanation is that I was made for another world."[171]

---

[170] Peter Kreeft and Ronald Tacelli, *Handbook of Christian Apologetics* (Downer's Grove, Ill: Intervarsity, 1994), p. 135.

[171] C.S. Lewis, *Mere Christianity,* from *The Complete C.S. Lewis Signature Classics* (New York: Harper One, 2002) (orig. 1952), p. 114.

It must be said, however, that this *argument from desire*, as it's usually called, is not well favored among philosophers and theologians. John Beversluis analyzed and rebutted Lewis' version of the argument in detail, for instance, in *C.S. Lewis and the Search for Rational Religion*, a mostly well-received analysis. (I recall an editor openly discouraging me from submitting material from this chapter for publication, because, he said, "Arguments from desire are not taken seriously enough by philosophers of religion...for there to be much literature on them.") Even Arend Smilde, a Lewis scholar and devotee, would be happy to see the argument from desire go away:

> Fifty years after the death of C. S. Lewis and some twenty-five years after the concept of a philosophical 'argument from desire' for the existence of God emerged in discussions of his work, this supposed argument now enjoys the status of a characteristic element in Lewis's intellectual legacy. However, as I want to show, the very concept of such an argument as an authentic part of that legacy needs to be scrapped if the real and important elements concealed by it are to recapture the light they deserve.[172]

Supposing that Smilde's critique is sound, we are still left with the question: just what is it that compels human beings to desire and expect so much more from life than what life actually has to offer? Evolutionary naturalism again does not provide much of an explanation. On evolutionary naturalism, organisms like ourselves exist only to survive (though it's never been explained to me how or why an incidental arrangement of inanimate chemicals would suddenly acquire an "instinct to survive" – let alone the ability to reproduce, metabolize, etc.). But survival in an evolutionary context requires no *hope*, i.e., no desire or expectation of a life that is better in some way to life as it actually is presently; it only requires doing what is necessary to stay alive in the short term. Beyond perhaps the

---

[172] Arend Smilde, "Horrid red herrings: A new look at the 'Lewisian Argument from Desire' – and beyond," *Journal of Inklings Studies*, Vol. 4, No. 1 (April 2014), p. 34.

psychological resilience necessary for recovering from life-threatening illnesses and the like, hope has no discernible survival function. (Otherwise it would almost seem to follow that extremely fast-breeding organisms like bacteria, say, or German cockroaches are also extremely *hopeful*.)

What I propose here is that the persistent desire for a better life – or alternatively, the persistent *dissatisfaction* with life as we currently live it – is not so much the premise of a sound deductive argument but a phenomenon crying out for explanation; and that the best explanation on offer is in fact the answer provided by Christian theology. This indeed is how Lewis himself framed the issue – as "the most probable explanation." With Lewis, I think Christianity best explains our dissonant psychological condition, not only as evidence of the fall of man, which beset humanity with pain and thrust him out of the Garden, but as evidence of the genuine hope that is still available to us through Jesus Christ. In the same way that Paradise Lost makes sense of our present condition, Paradise Regained makes sense of our stubborn, irrational insistence on believing that one day our lives will not just be better, but incomparably better than anything we've experienced to date.

The Hope of the Gospel

Christianity points us to the cross, where justice and mercy converge. On the cross Jesus not only pays the penalty demanded by justice and offers humanity forgiveness of sins (evils) committed through abuse of moral freedom, but promises the reward of the just: hope of eternal life in the kingdom of heaven. This is the "good news" of the gospel, really the greatest news there could possibly be:

> Jesus' life-death-resurrection-exaltation undoes what has happened to Adam and Israel. God's new world is launched in the midst of the old one. The insidious powers of desire, death, and the devil receive their fatal blow in the cross of Christ and his glorious resurrection. The gospel marks the beginning of paradise restored.[173]

Glorious as the promise of paradise restored may be, God has seen fit to retain for us the freedom to accept or refuse this gospel of grace. Christian

---

[173] Bird, p. 492-3.

theology therefore best explains the concurrence of our most basic desires: both the desire for unceasing happiness and the desire for moral autonomy.

By this reading, the purpose of human existence on earth is to make eternally binding decisions to accept or refuse God's offer of everlasting life in the kingdom of heaven, through either self-denying faith in Christ or self-seeking unbelief. Or as Neo put it to the Architect of the Matrix: "The problem is choice." That is, the perceived dichotomy of hope and evil reveals that we simply can't have everything we want. More than choice, then, the problem is *desire*. As humans beset with a corrupt nature spiritually transmitted through the fall of Adam, we cannot choose to be righteous or sinless. However, there is nothing stopping us from choosing to *desire* it – to "hunger and thirst for righteousness" and to "seek first the kingdom of God," as Jesus said. Our purpose, therefore, in this sometimes dangerous and heartbreaking, sometimes exciting and beautiful world, may be to simply decide what it is we really want. And so the wisdom of Christ calls:

> "For whoever desires to save his life will lose it, but whoever loses his life for My sake and the gospel's will save it. For what will it profit a man if he gains the whole world, and loses his own soul? Or what will a man give in exchange for his soul?" (Mark 8:35-37).

www.ingramcontent.com/pod-product-compliance
Lightning Source LLC
Chambersburg PA
CBHW061646040426
42446CB00010B/1598